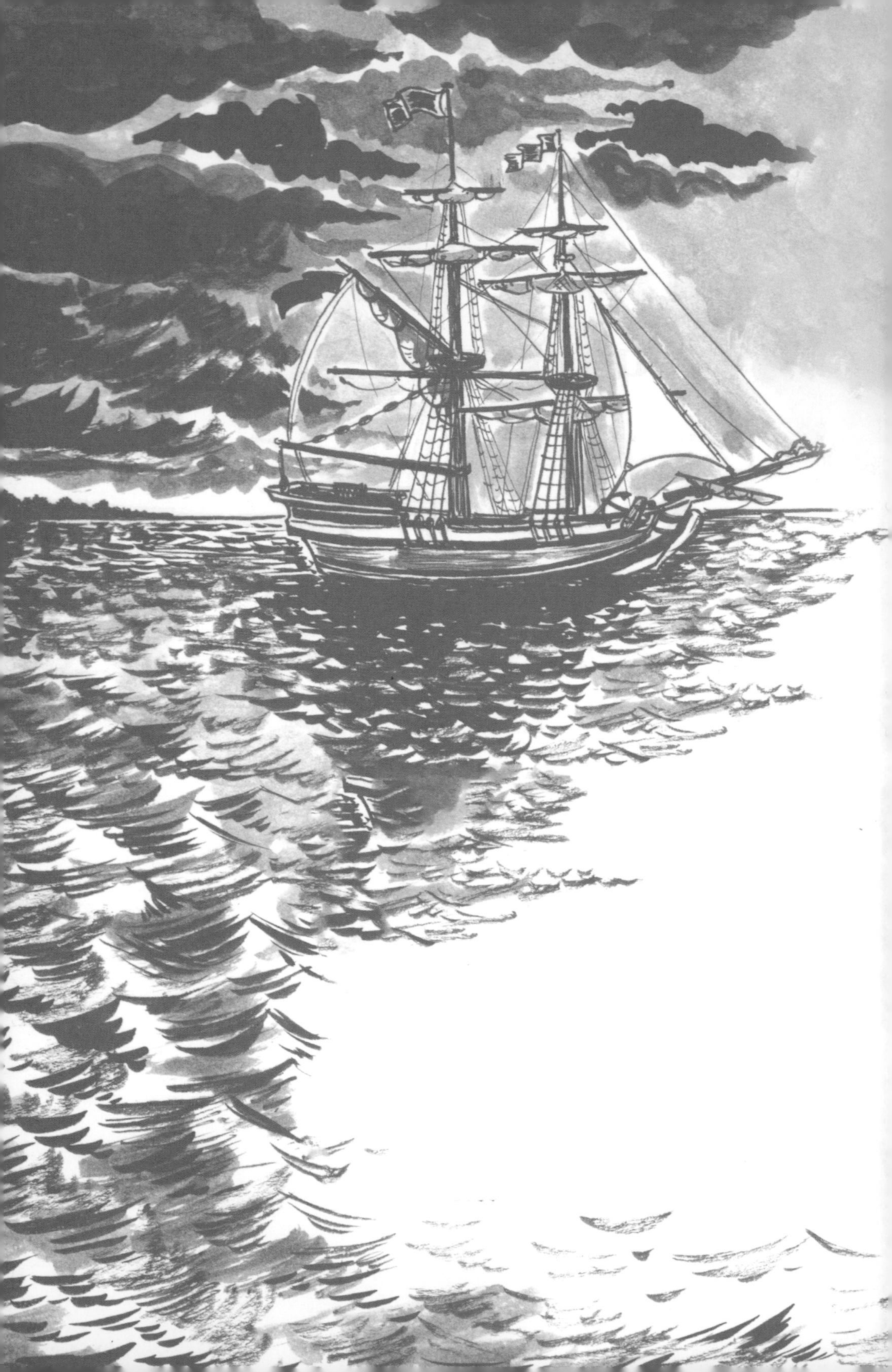

BAGGYWRINKLES

A Lubber's Guide to Life at Sea

created by
Lucy Bellwood

art
Lucy Bellwood

colors
Joey Weiser and Michele Chidester

book design
Allyson Haller

Published in the United States by Elea Press / Lucy Bellwood
Second edition: January 2017
ISBN: 978-0-9882202-9-4

Graphic Novels / History / Autobiography

Cover Illustration by Lucy Bellwood

Printed in Malaysia

TABLE of CONTENTS

Introduction
» 07 «

Strips

The Call of the Running Tide » 09

What is a Baggywrinkle? » 21

Sea of Ink » 23

Fathom Fact » 35

Parts Unknown » 37

Hard Tack » 59

The Plank » 61

Pacific Passages » 77

Glossary » 93

Scurvy Dogs » 95

Scurvy Afterword
» 115 «

Guest Art Gallery
» 119 to 128 «

INTRODUCTION

> **At the tender age of seventeen I ran away to sea.**

Okay, maybe not "ran away." My parents dropped me off at the airport. I flew to northern California. I spent two weeks crewing aboard the tall ship *Lady Washington* and it changed my life forever.

The *Lady Washington* is a fully-functional replica of a Boston-built brig active in the tea trade circuit of the 1790s. She looks as one would imagine a pirate ship to look, though her crew are quick to remind you that they're not pirates—they're merchant mariners. Pirates are jerks.

Crewing on the *Lady* was just a gateway to the wider world of modern tall ship sailing—a profession I would've doubtless aspired to from infancy if I'd had any idea it was still a career option. As a kid with no sailing experience whatsoever, the first two weeks I spent aboard were a staggering deluge of information and adrenaline. Trying to learn the names of 114 distinct lines while quelling my anxiety about working 86 feet off the deck on the t'gallant yard was no small feat, but I left completely intoxicated with the crew, the lifestyle, and the impossible realness of it all.

In the years that followed I went back whenever I had the chance—summers and winters, balmy days and stormy nights—to furl sails and haul halyards and sing shanties with an ever-changing crew. I worked on other vessels. I went away to college. And when I fell into drawing comics in 2010 it seemed an obvious choice to visually try and explain this surreal world I inhabited where the past was alive and well in the present.

Baggywrinkles, named for the fluffy and oft-commented-upon anti-chafing devices in a ship's rigging, became an outlet for all the fascinating nautical ephemera I'd picked up during my time at sea. It's partly an account of my experiences as a deckhand, but mostly a chance to share the entertaining, esoteric, and downright strange historical facts of life at sea.

If it inspires you to run away as well, so much the better. I look forward to swapping stories in a future port.

Fair Winds and Following Seas,

Lucy Bellwood

THE CALL OF THE RUNNING TIDE

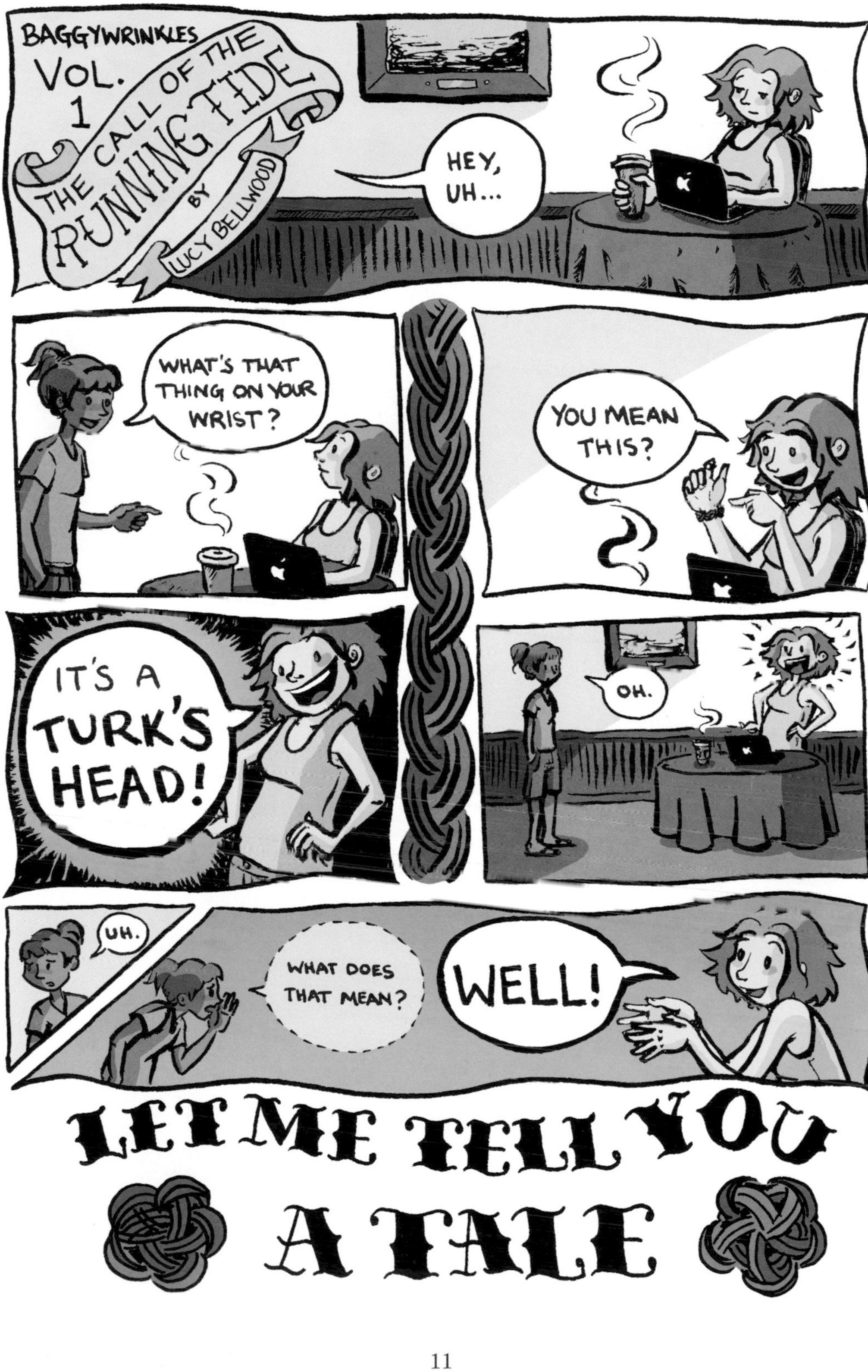
BAGGYWRINKLES
VOL. 1
THE CALL OF THE RUNNING TIDE
BY LUCY BELLWOOD
HEY, UH...
WHAT'S THAT THING ON YOUR WRIST?
YOU MEAN THIS?
IT'S A TURK'S HEAD!
OH.
UH.
WHAT DOES THAT MEAN?
WELL!
LET ME TELL YOU A TALE

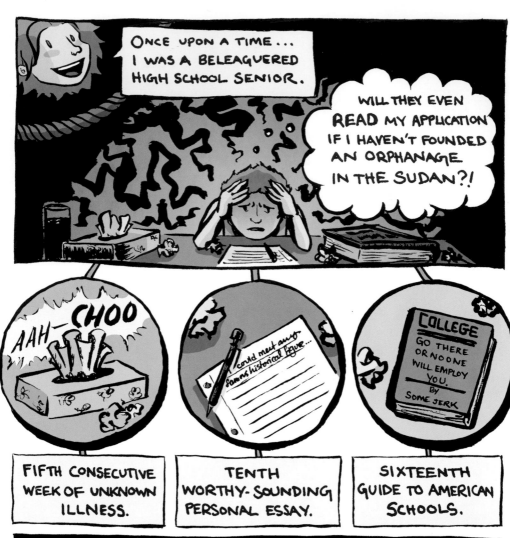

ONCE UPON A TIME...
I WAS A BELEAGUERED
HIGH SCHOOL SENIOR.

WILL THEY EVEN
READ MY APPLICATION
IF I HAVEN'T FOUNDED
AN ORPHANAGE
IN THE SUDAN?!

AAH— CHOO

could meet any
famous historical figure...

COLLEGE
GO THERE
OR NO ONE
WILL EMPLOY
YOU.
BY
SOME JERK

FIFTH CONSECUTIVE
WEEK OF UNKNOWN
ILLNESS.

TENTH
WORTHY-SOUNDING
PERSONAL ESSAY.

SIXTEENTH
GUIDE TO AMERICAN
SCHOOLS.

AND LIKE ANY HIGH SCHOOL STUDENT,
I WAS VERY EFFECTIVE AT USING
THE INTERNET...

OOOOOOH.

...FOR PROCRASTINATION.

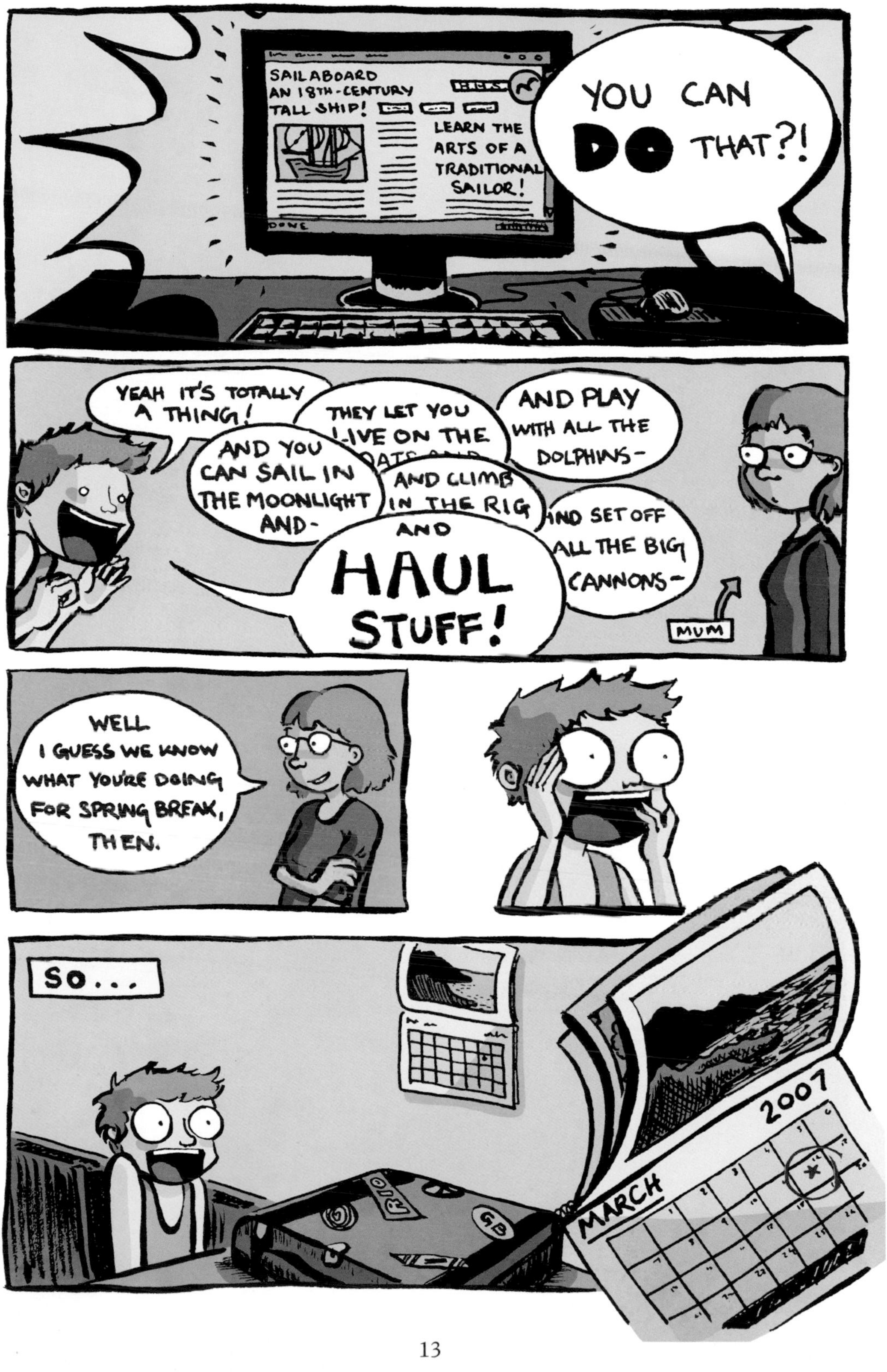
SAILABOARD AN 18TH-CENTURY TALL SHIP!
LEARN THE ARTS OF A TRADITIONAL SAILOR!
DONE
YOU CAN DO THAT?!
YEAH IT'S TOTALLY A THING!
THEY LET YOU LIVE ON THE
AND PLAY WITH ALL THE DOLPHINS-
AND YOU CAN SAIL IN THE MOONLIGHT AND-
AND CLIMB IN THE RIG
ND SET OFF ALL THE BIG CANNONS-
AND HAUL STUFF!
MUM
WELL I GUESS WE KNOW WHAT YOU'RE DOING FOR SPRING BREAK, THEN.
SO...
RIO
GB
2007
MARCH

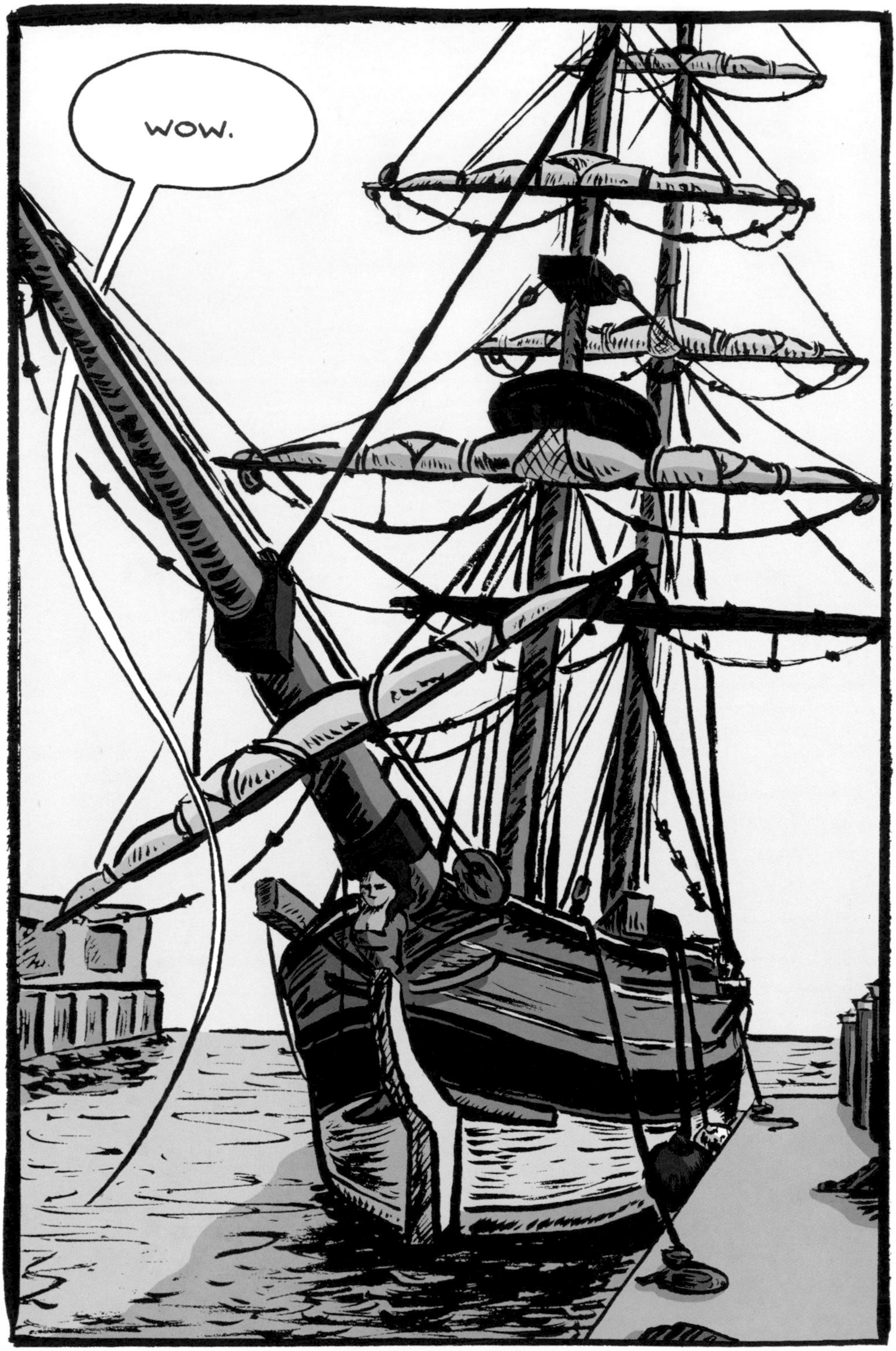
WOW.

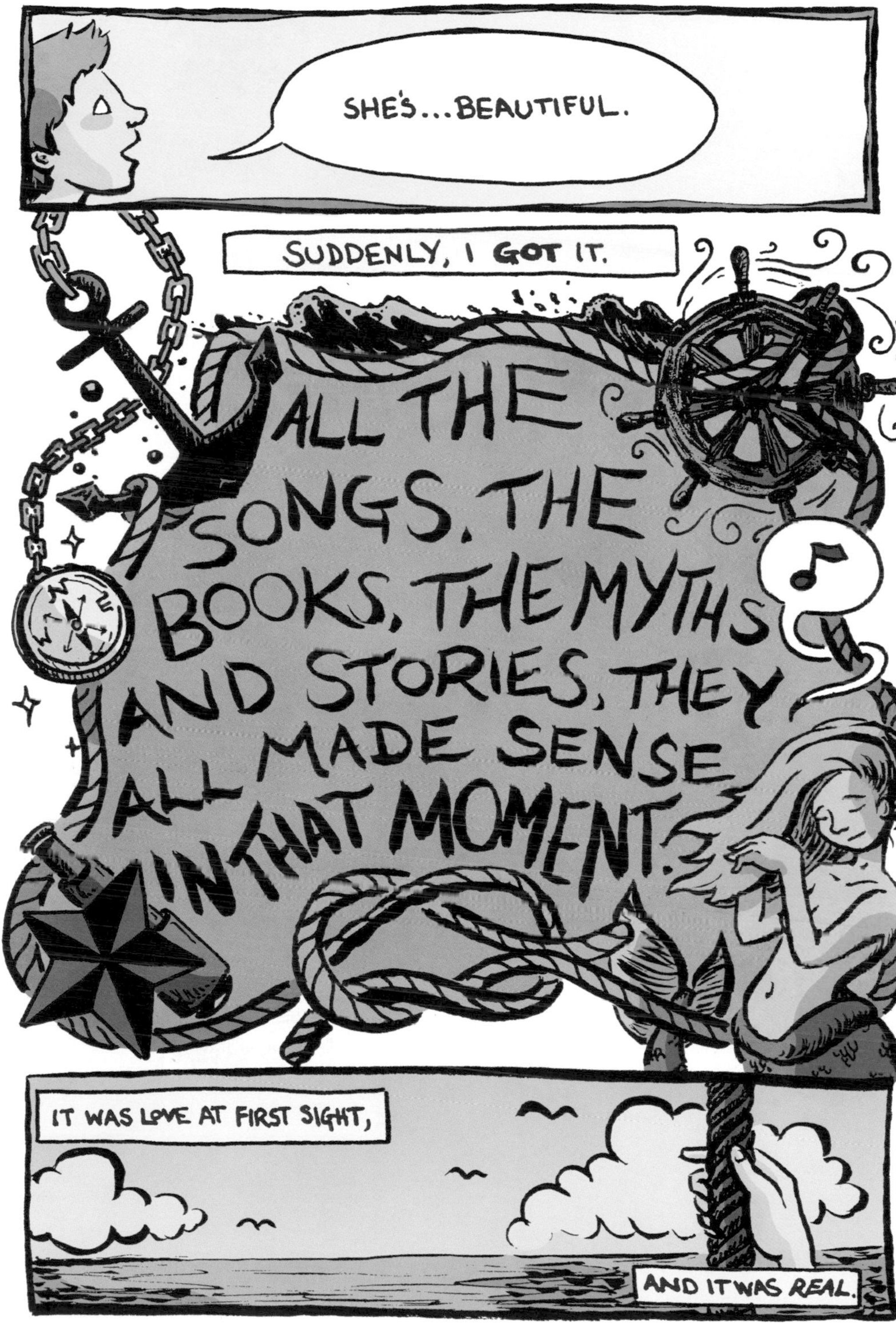
SHE'S...BEAUTIFUL.
SUDDENLY, I GOT IT.
ALL THE SONGS, THE BOOKS, THE MYTHS AND STORIES, THEY ALL MADE SENSE IN THAT MOMENT.
IT WAS LOVE AT FIRST SIGHT,
AND IT WAS *REAL*.

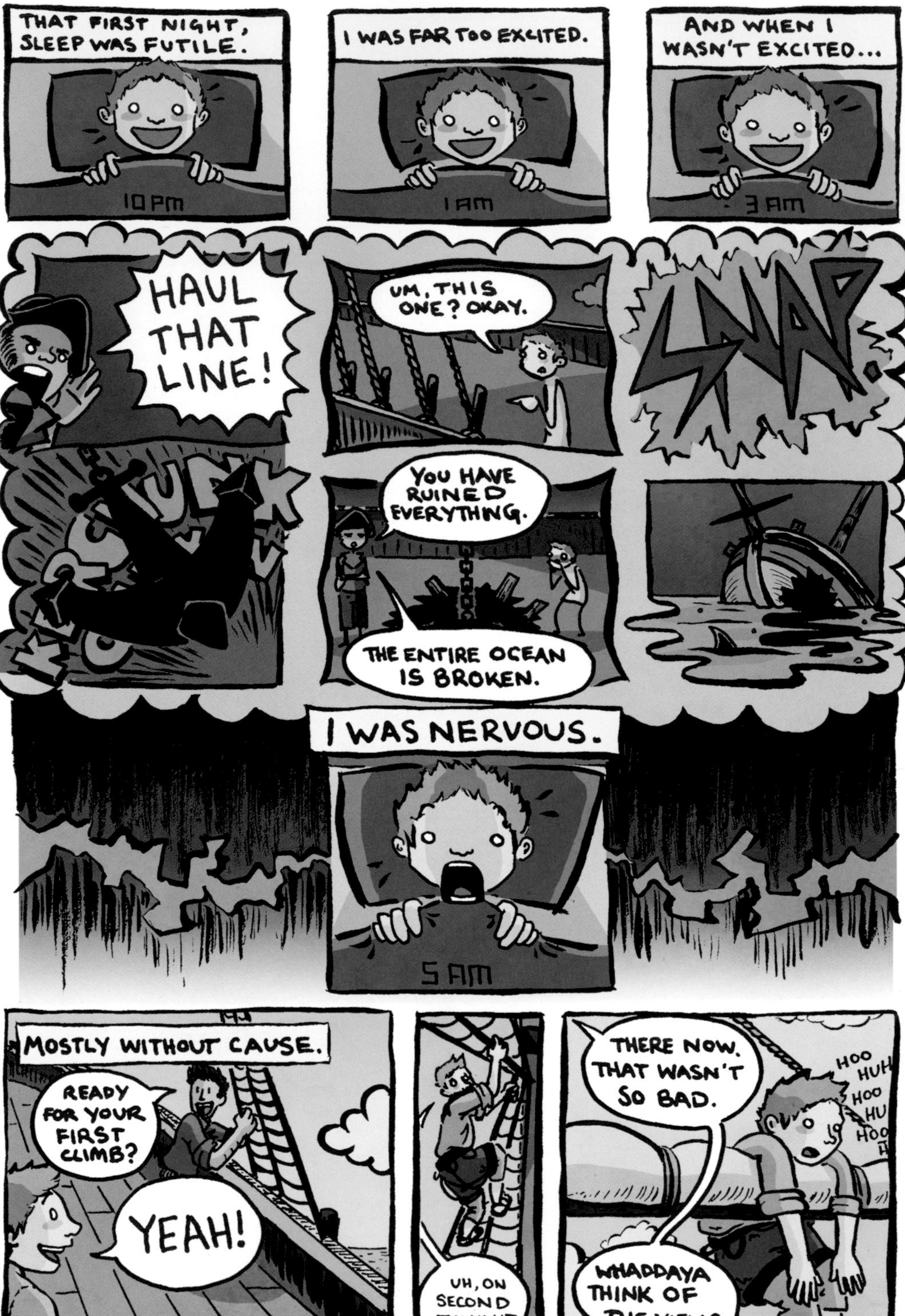
THAT FIRST NIGHT, SLEEP WAS FUTILE.
10 PM
I WAS FAR TOO EXCITED.
1 AM
AND WHEN I WASN'T EXCITED...
3 AM
HAUL THAT LINE!
UM, THIS ONE? OKAY.
SNAP.
YOU HAVE RUINED EVERYTHING.
THE ENTIRE OCEAN IS BROKEN.
I WAS NERVOUS.
5 AM
MOSTLY WITHOUT CAUSE.
READY FOR YOUR FIRST CLIMB?
YEAH!
UH, ON SECOND THOUGHT...
THERE NOW. THAT WASN'T SO BAD.
HOO HUH HOO HU HOO H
WHADDAYA THINK OF THE VIEW?

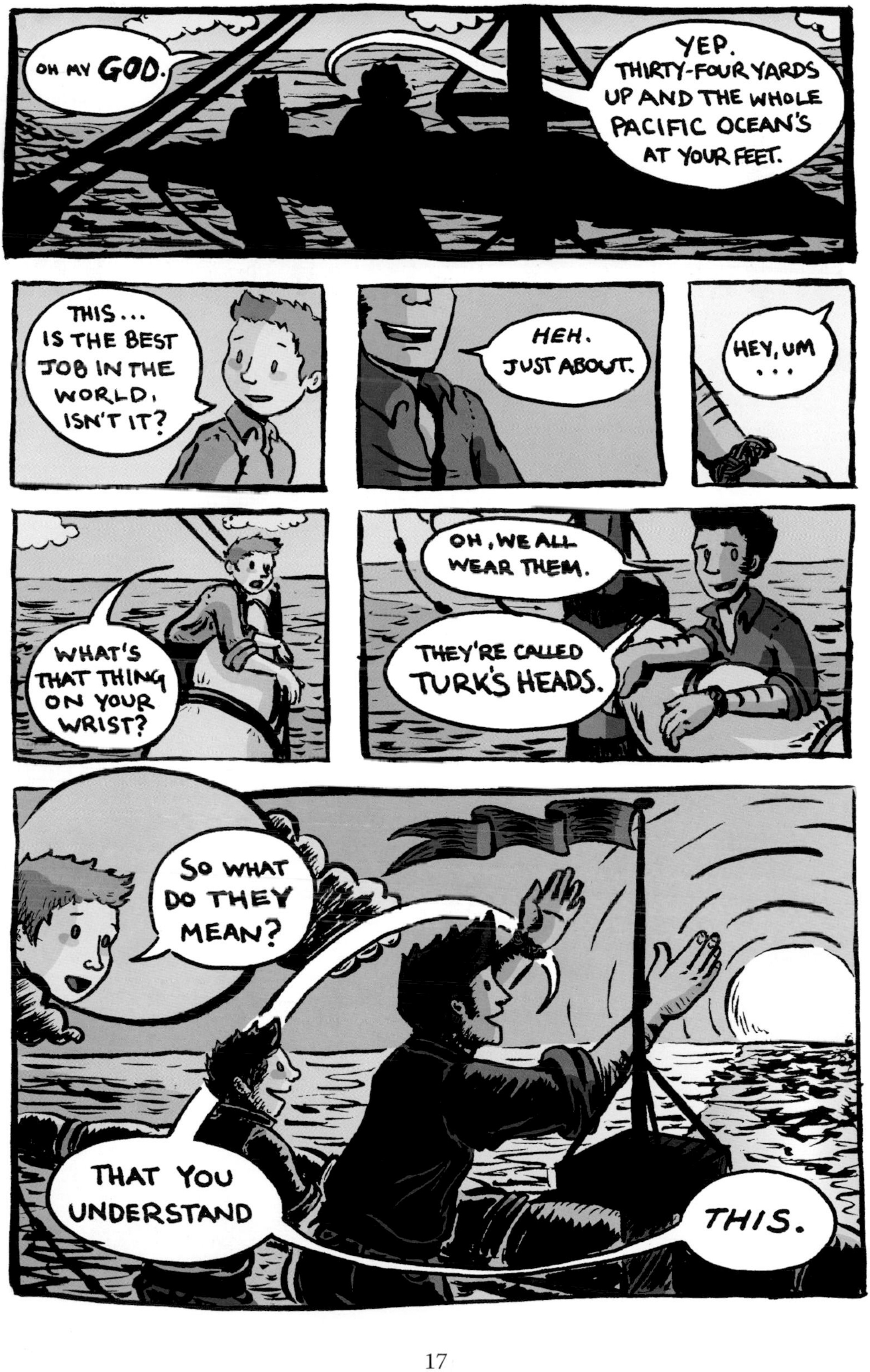
OH MY GOD.
YEP. THIRTY-FOUR YARDS UP AND THE WHOLE PACIFIC OCEAN'S AT YOUR FEET.
THIS... IS THE BEST JOB IN THE WORLD, ISN'T IT?
HEH. JUST ABOUT.
HEY, UM ...
WHAT'S THAT THING ON YOUR WRIST?
OH, WE ALL WEAR THEM.
THEY'RE CALLED TURK'S HEADS.
SO WHAT DO THEY MEAN?
THAT YOU UNDERSTAND
THIS.

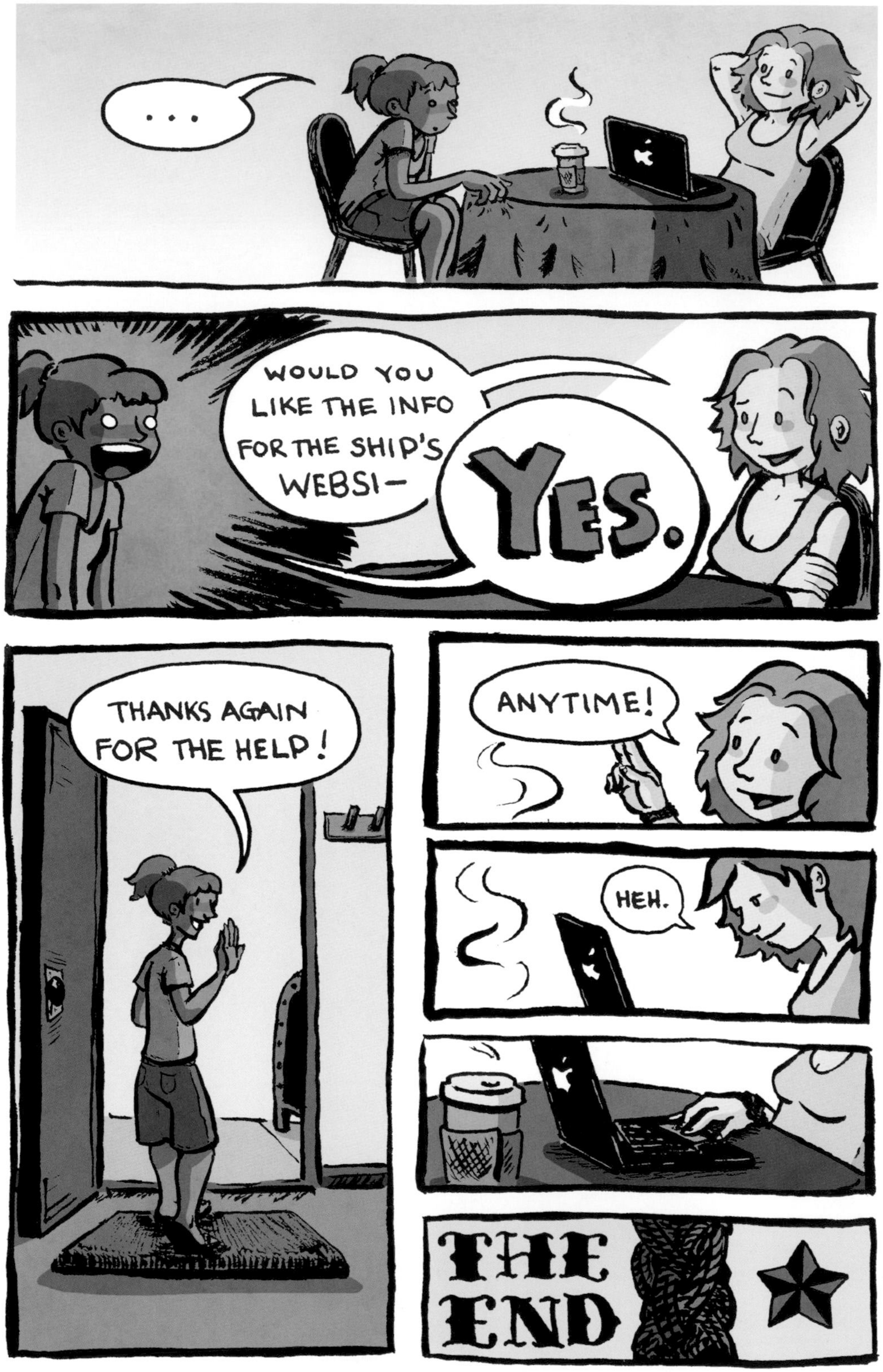
...
WOULD YOU LIKE THE INFO FOR THE SHIP'S WEBSI-
YES.
THANKS AGAIN FOR THE HELP!
ANYTIME!
HEH.
THE END

WHAT IS A BAGGYWRINKLE?

The first thing people generally say when they set foot on a tall ship is...

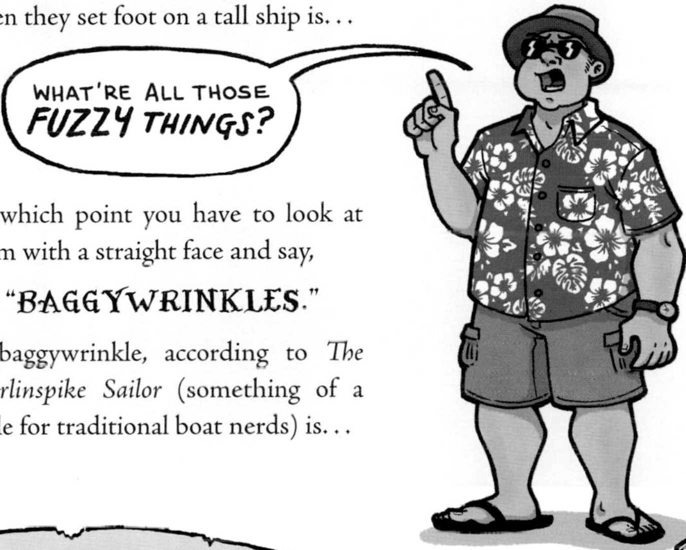
WHAT'RE ALL THOSE FUZZY THINGS?

At which point you have to look at them with a straight face and say,

"BAGGYWRINKLES."

A baggywrinkle, according to *The Marlinspike Sailor* (something of a bible for traditional boat nerds) is...

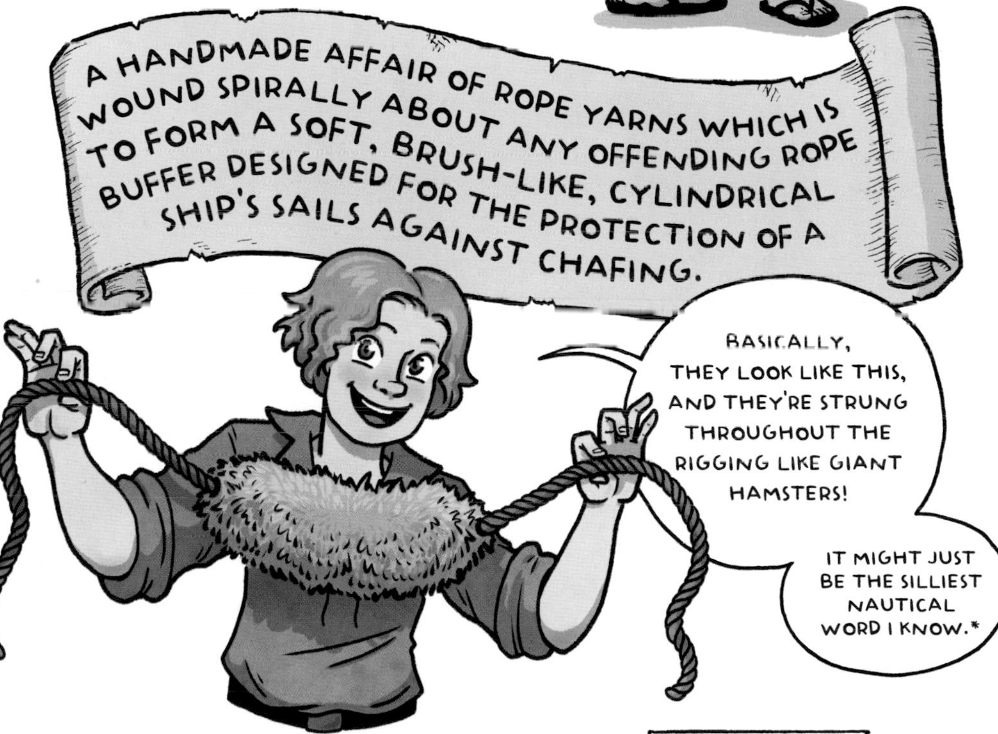
A HANDMADE AFFAIR OF ROPE YARNS WHICH IS WOUND SPIRALLY ABOUT ANY OFFENDING ROPE TO FORM A SOFT, BRUSH-LIKE, CYLINDRICAL BUFFER DESIGNED FOR THE PROTECTION OF A SHIP'S SAILS AGAINST CHAFING.
BASICALLY, THEY LOOK LIKE THIS, AND THEY'RE STRUNG THROUGHOUT THE RIGGING LIKE GIANT HAMSTERS!
IT MIGHT JUST BE THE SILLIEST NAUTICAL WORD I KNOW.*

* This is not true.

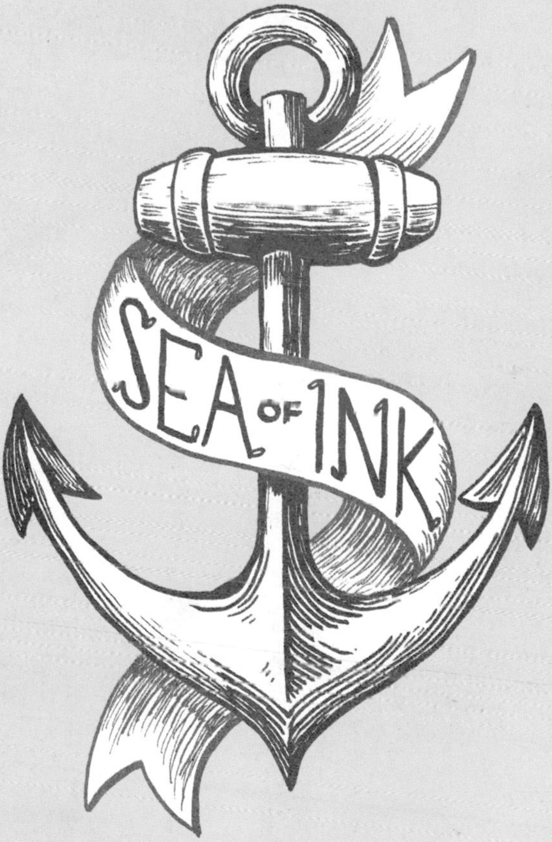
SEA OF INK

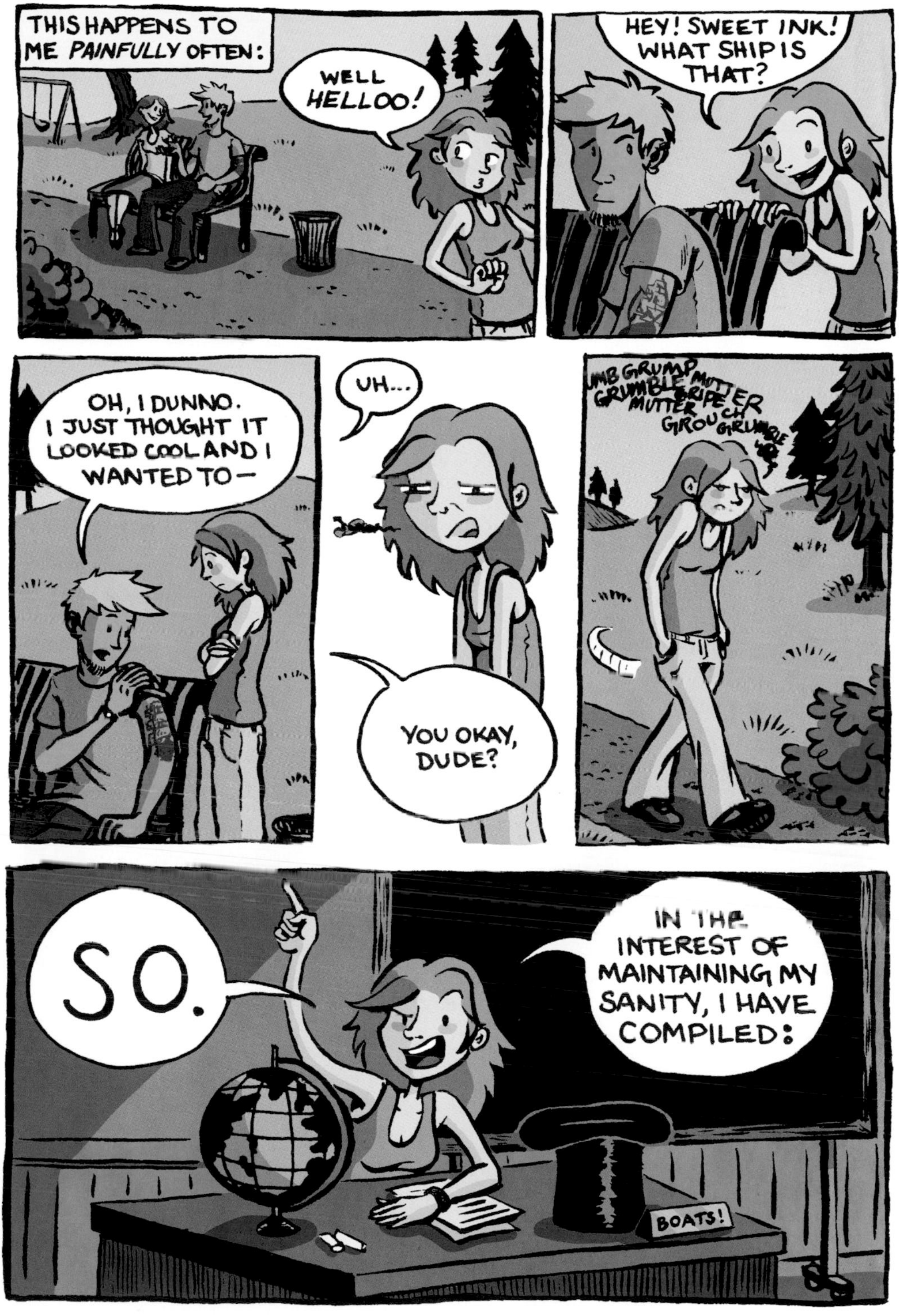

THIS HAPPENS TO ME *PAINFULLY* OFTEN:
WELL HELLOO!
HEY! SWEET INK! WHAT SHIP IS THAT?
OH, I DUNNO. I JUST THOUGHT IT LOOKED COOL AND I WANTED TO—
UH...
YOU OKAY, DUDE?
UMB GRUMP GRUMBLE MUTTER GRIPE MUTTER GROUCH
SO.
IN THE INTEREST OF MAINTAINING MY SANITY, I HAVE COMPILED:
BOATS!

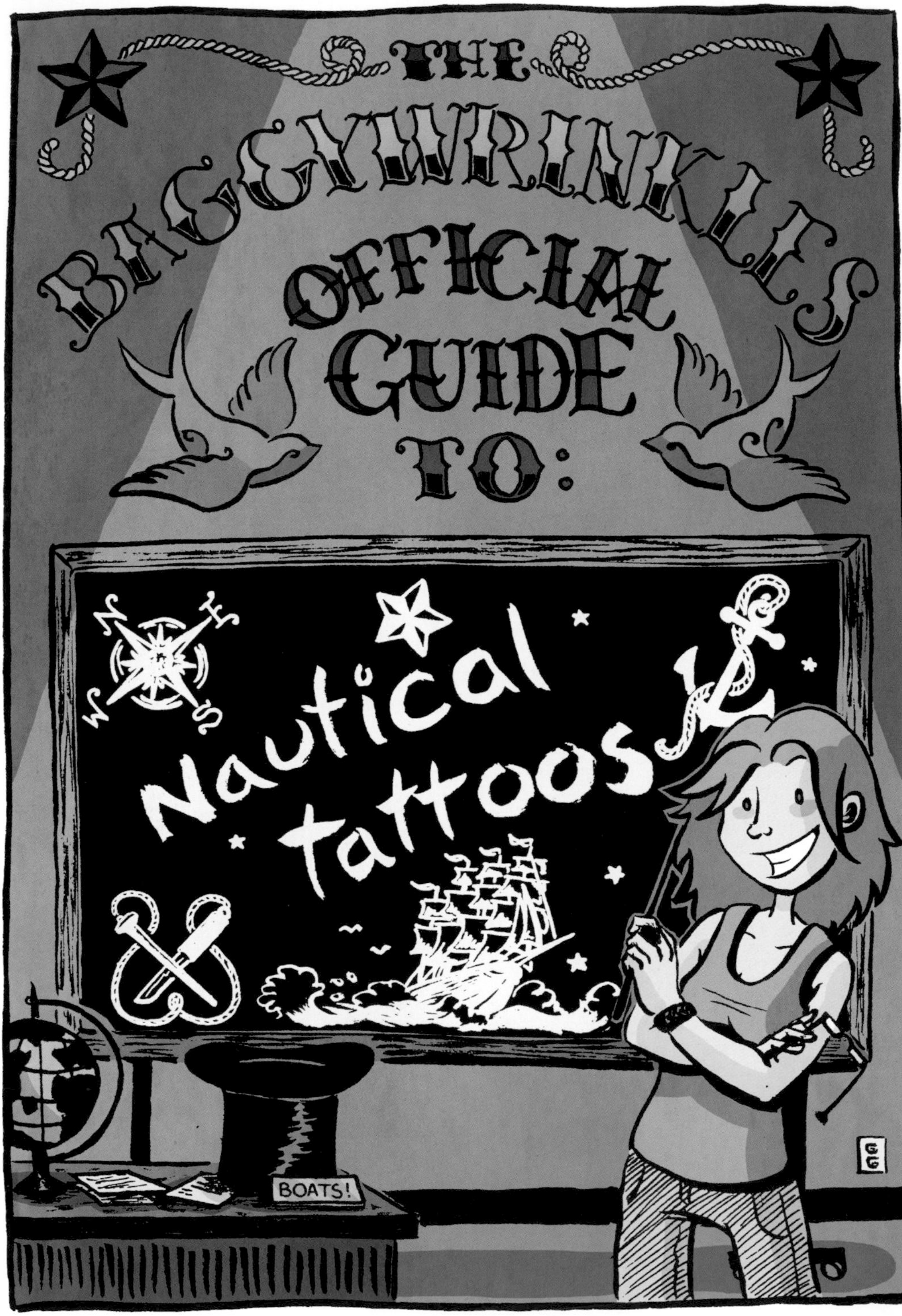
THE
BAGGYWRINKLES
OFFICIAL
GUIDE
TO:
Nautical tattoos
N
E
W
S
BOATS!
GG

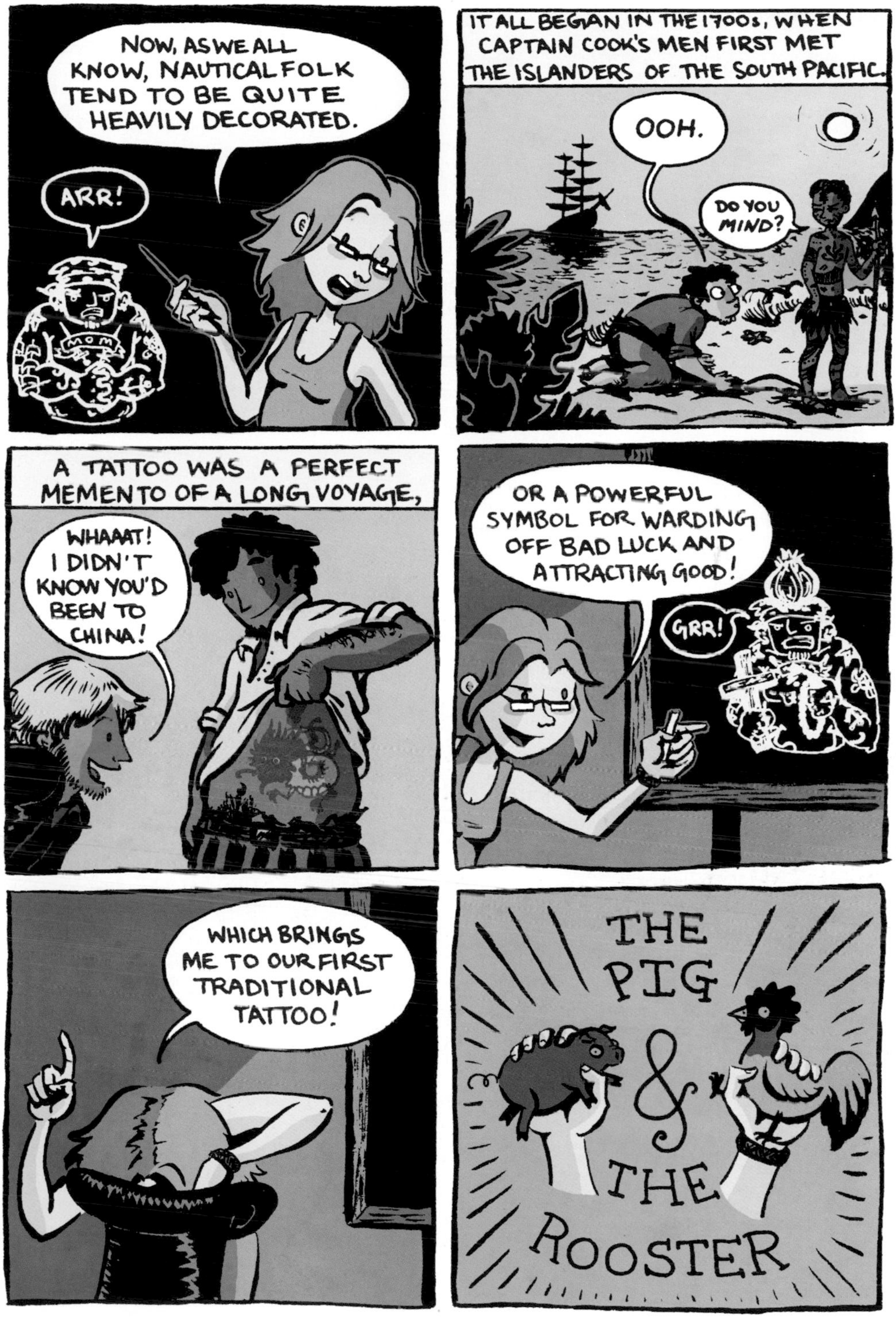
NOW, AS WE ALL KNOW, NAUTICAL FOLK TEND TO BE QUITE HEAVILY DECORATED.
ARR!
MOM
IT ALL BEGAN IN THE 1700s, WHEN CAPTAIN COOK'S MEN FIRST MET THE ISLANDERS OF THE SOUTH PACIFIC.
OOH.
DO YOU MIND?
A TATTOO WAS A PERFECT MEMENTO OF A LONG VOYAGE,
WHAAAT! I DIDN'T KNOW YOU'D BEEN TO CHINA!
OR A POWERFUL SYMBOL FOR WARDING OFF BAD LUCK AND ATTRACTING GOOD!
GRR!
WHICH BRINGS ME TO OUR FIRST TRADITIONAL TATTOO!
THE PIG & THE ROOSTER

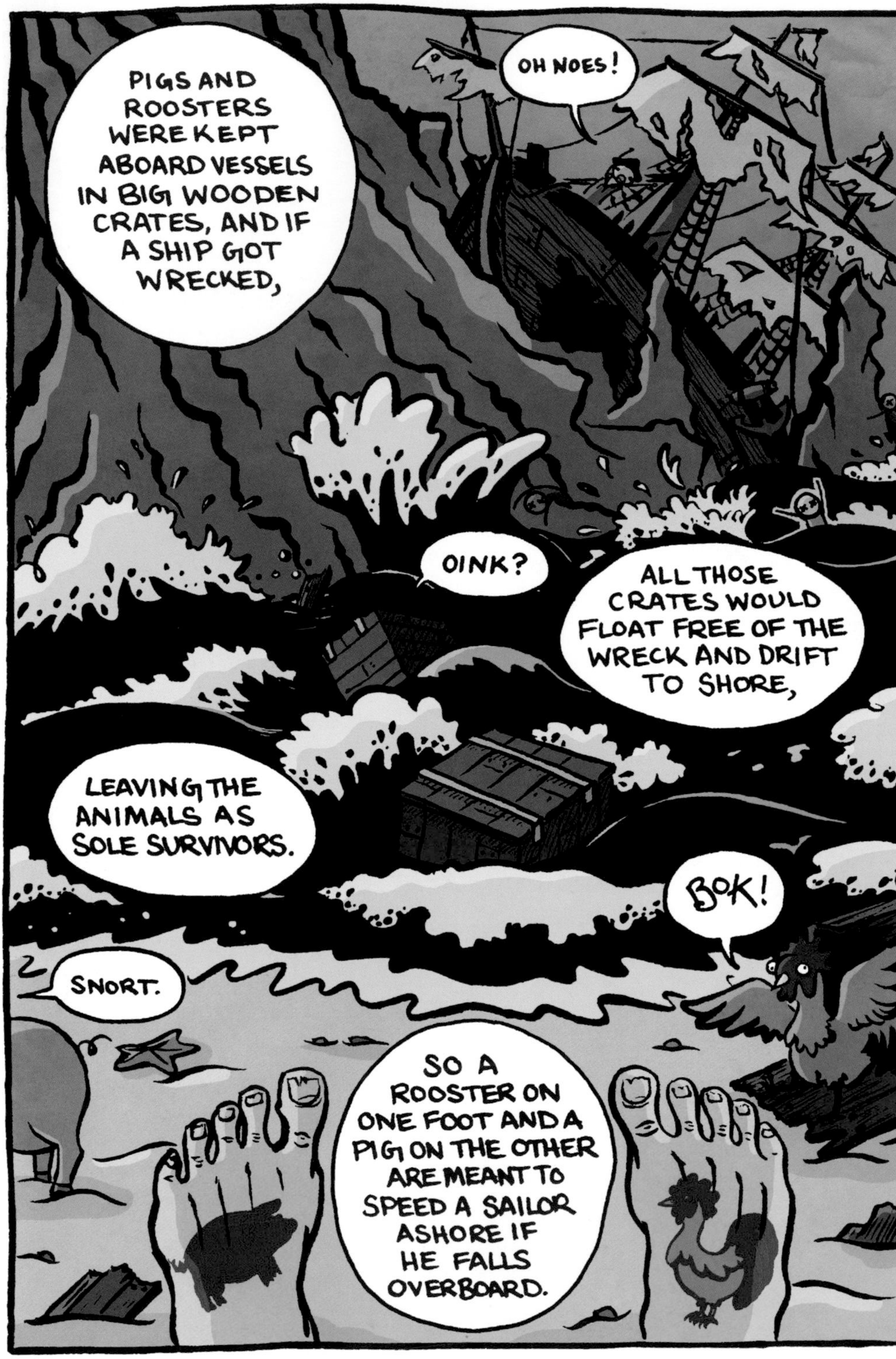
PIGS AND ROOSTERS WERE KEPT ABOARD VESSELS IN BIG WOODEN CRATES, AND IF A SHIP GOT WRECKED,
OH NOES!
OINK?
ALL THOSE CRATES WOULD FLOAT FREE OF THE WRECK AND DRIFT TO SHORE,
LEAVING THE ANIMALS AS SOLE SURVIVORS.
BOK!
SNORT.
SO A ROOSTER ON ONE FOOT AND A PIG ON THE OTHER ARE MEANT TO SPEED A SAILOR ASHORE IF HE FALLS OVERBOARD.

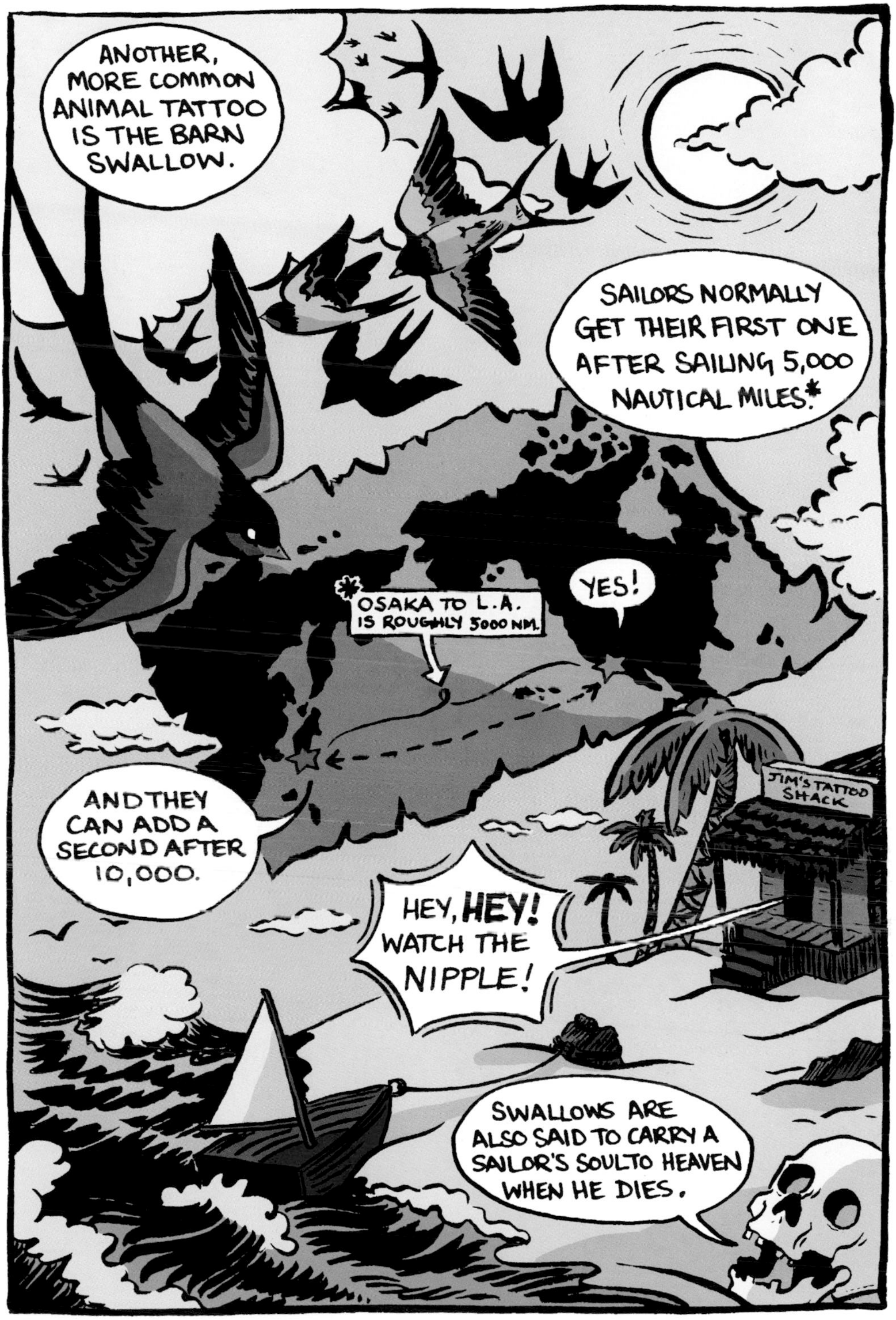
ANOTHER, MORE COMMON ANIMAL TATTOO IS THE BARN SWALLOW.
SAILORS NORMALLY GET THEIR FIRST ONE AFTER SAILING 5,000 NAUTICAL MILES.*
YES!
* OSAKA TO L.A. IS ROUGHLY 5000 NM.
AND THEY CAN ADD A SECOND AFTER 10,000.
JIM'S TATTOO SHACK
HEY, HEY! WATCH THE NIPPLE!
SWALLOWS ARE ALSO SAID TO CARRY A SAILOR'S SOUL TO HEAVEN WHEN HE DIES.

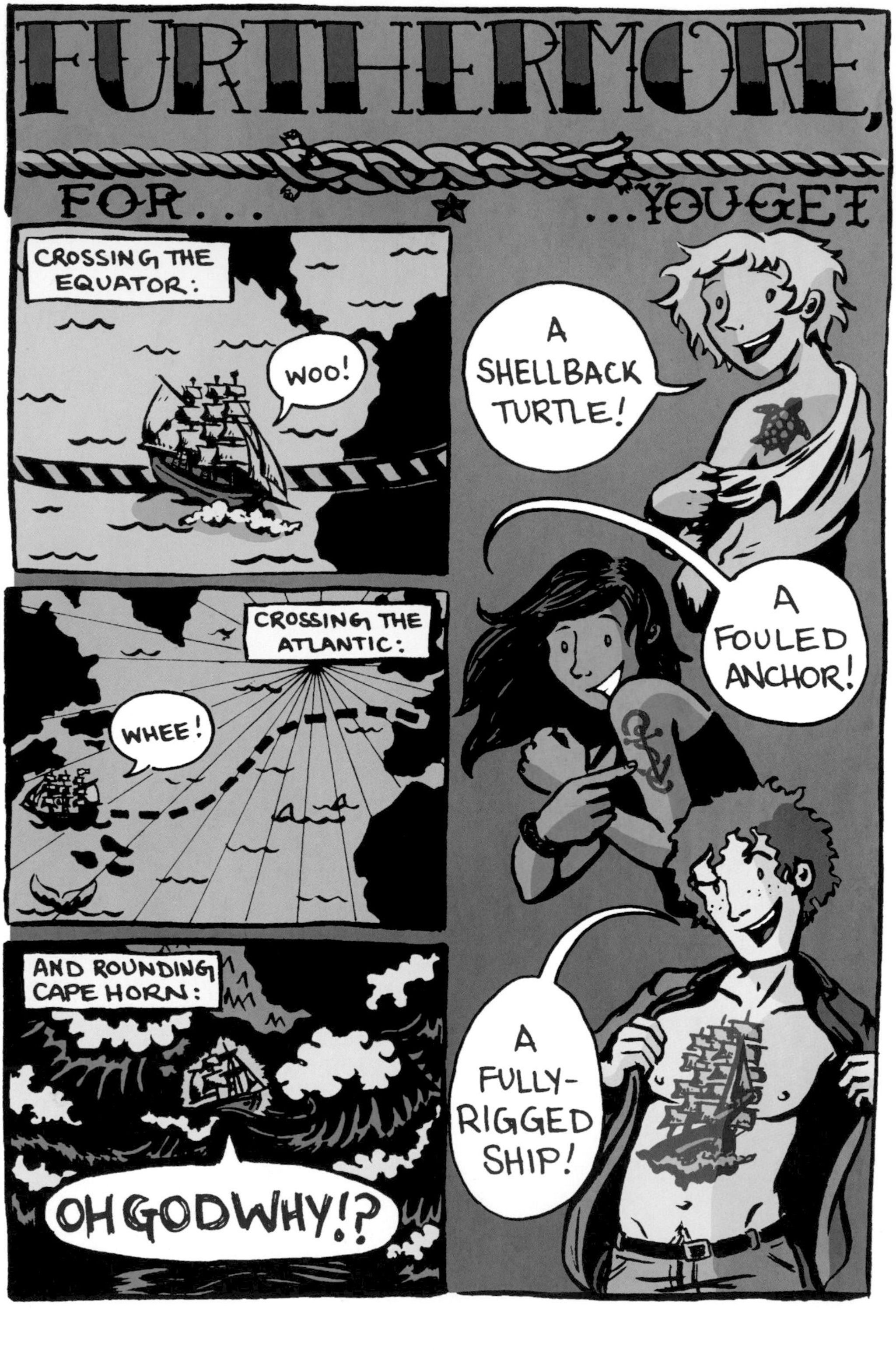
FURTHERMORE,
FOR...
...YOU GET
CROSSING THE EQUATOR:
WOO!
A SHELLBACK TURTLE!
CROSSING THE ATLANTIC:
WHEE!
A FOULED ANCHOR!
AND ROUNDING CAPE HORN:
OHGODWHY!?
A FULLY-RIGGED SHIP!

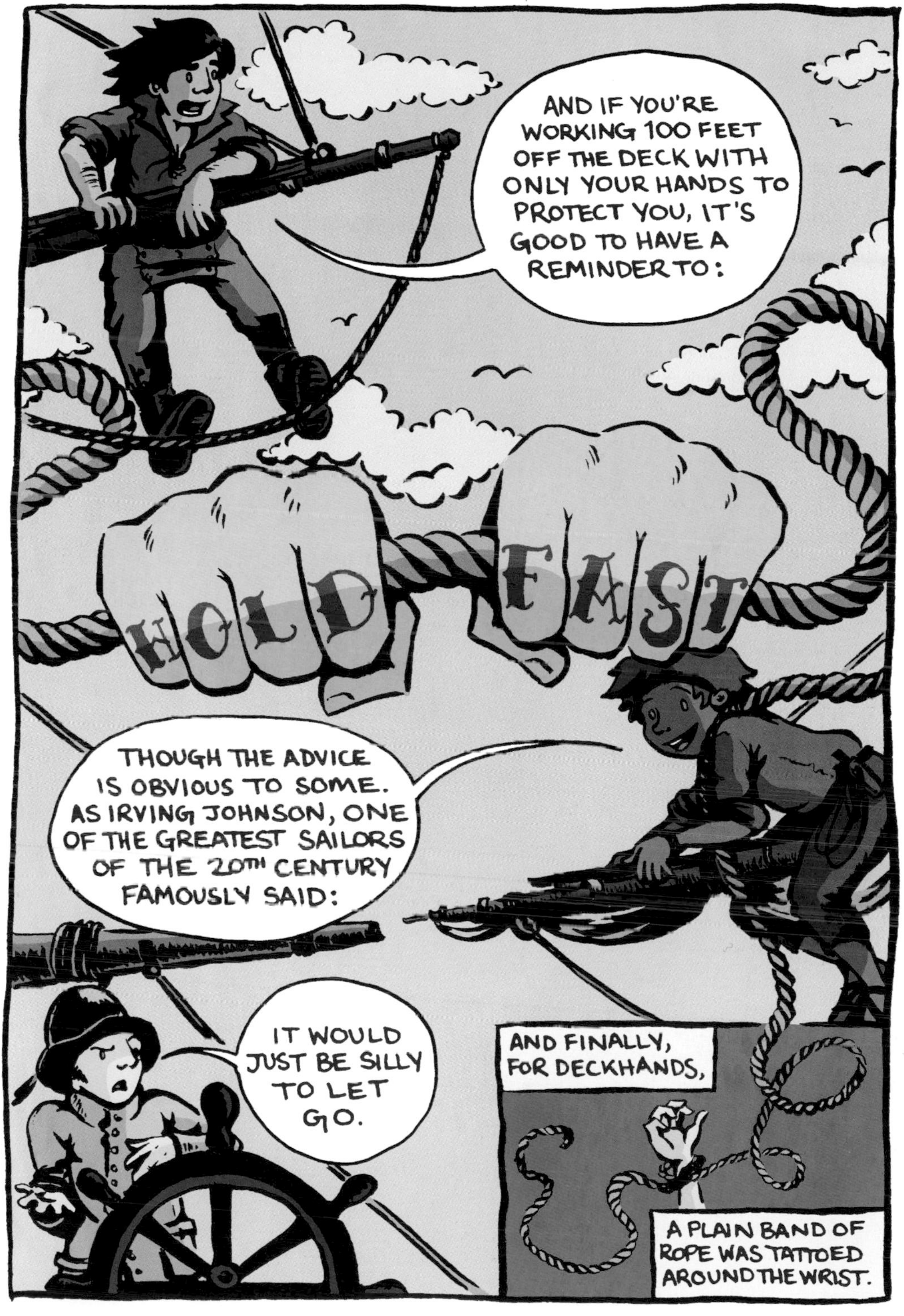
AND IF YOU'RE WORKING 100 FEET OFF THE DECK WITH ONLY YOUR HANDS TO PROTECT YOU, IT'S GOOD TO HAVE A REMINDER TO:
HOLD FAST
THOUGH THE ADVICE IS OBVIOUS TO SOME. AS IRVING JOHNSON, ONE OF THE GREATEST SAILORS OF THE 20TH CENTURY FAMOUSLY SAID:
IT WOULD JUST BE SILLY TO LET GO.
AND FINALLY, FOR DECKHANDS,
A PLAIN BAND OF ROPE WAS TATTOOED AROUND THE WRIST.

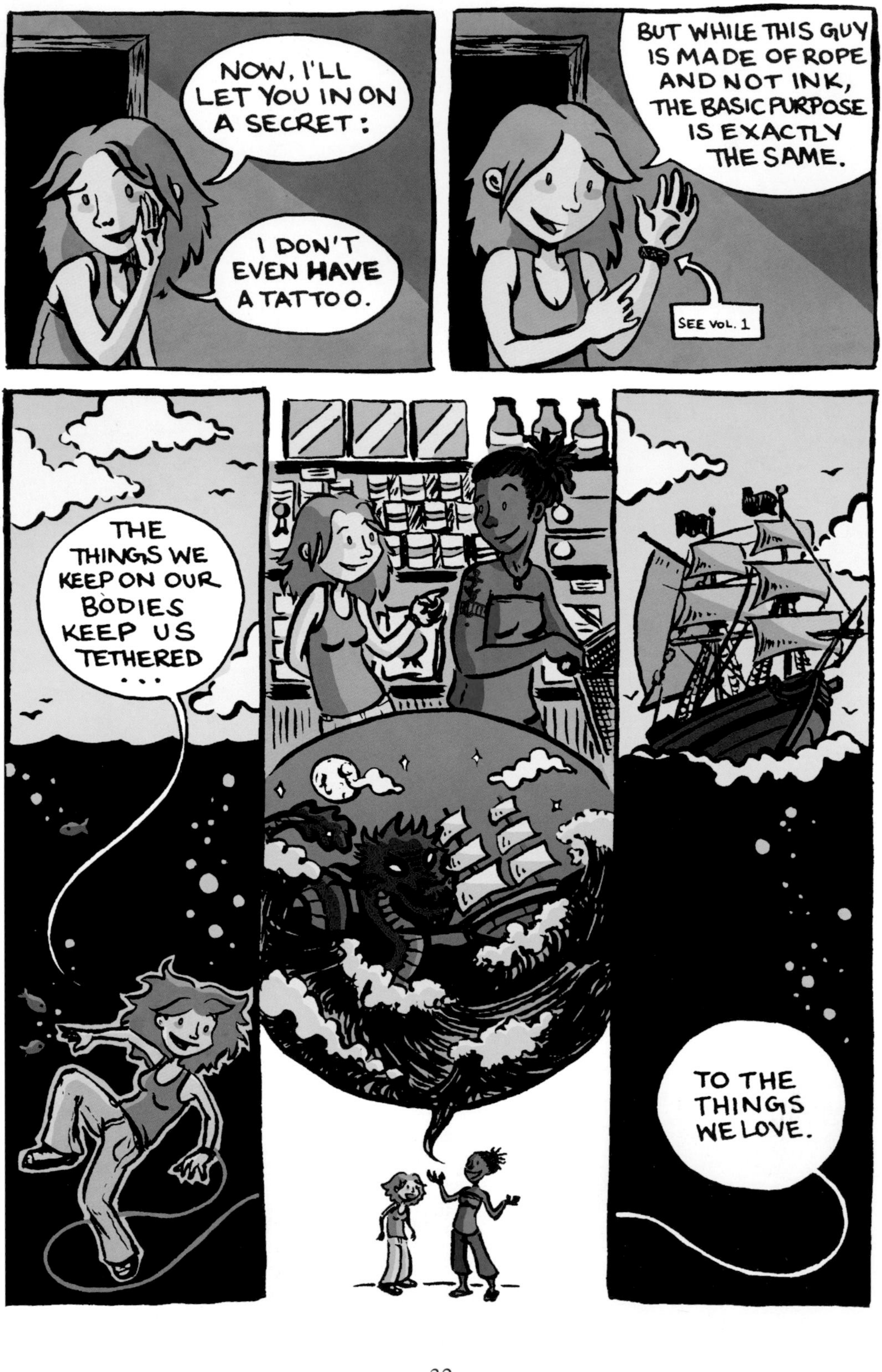
NOW, I'LL LET YOU IN ON A SECRET:
I DON'T EVEN HAVE A TATTOO.
BUT WHILE THIS GUY IS MADE OF ROPE AND NOT INK, THE BASIC PURPOSE IS EXACTLY THE SAME.
SEE VOL. 1
THE THINGS WE KEEP ON OUR BODIES KEEP US TETHERED . . .
TO THE THINGS WE LOVE.

FATHOM FACT

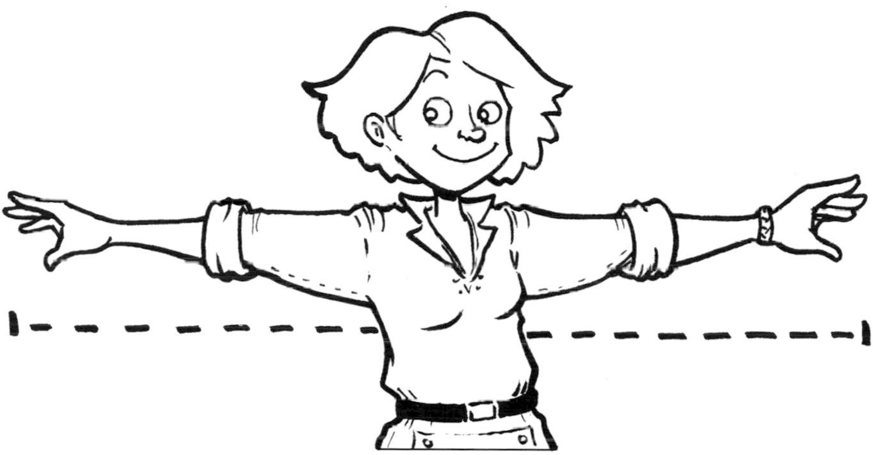

FATHOMS,
NOW STANDARDIZED AT
SIX FEET,
WERE ORIGINALLY DETERMINED BY
"THE LENGTH OF A MAN'S ARMS
AROUND THE OBJECT OF HIS
AFFECTIONS."

WHAT'S YOUR FATHOM?

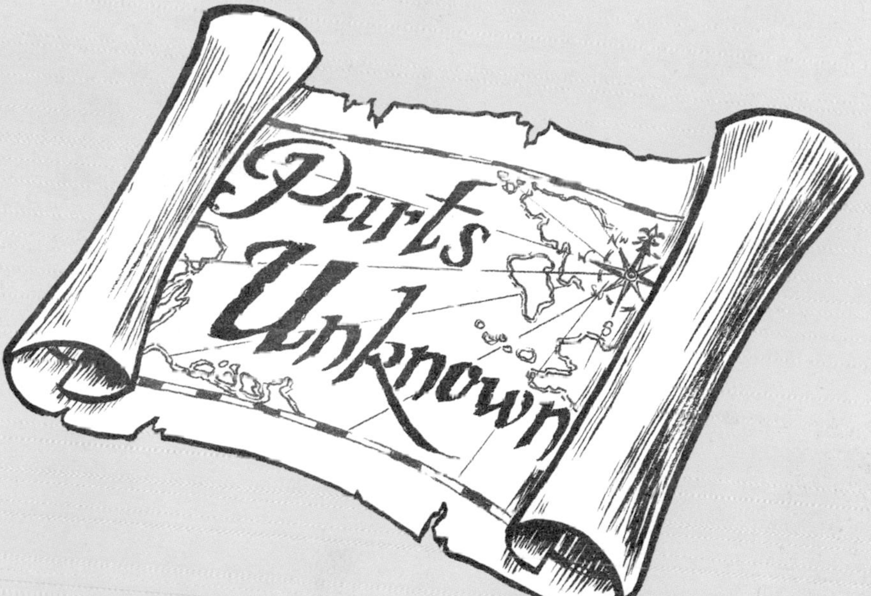
Parts
Unknown

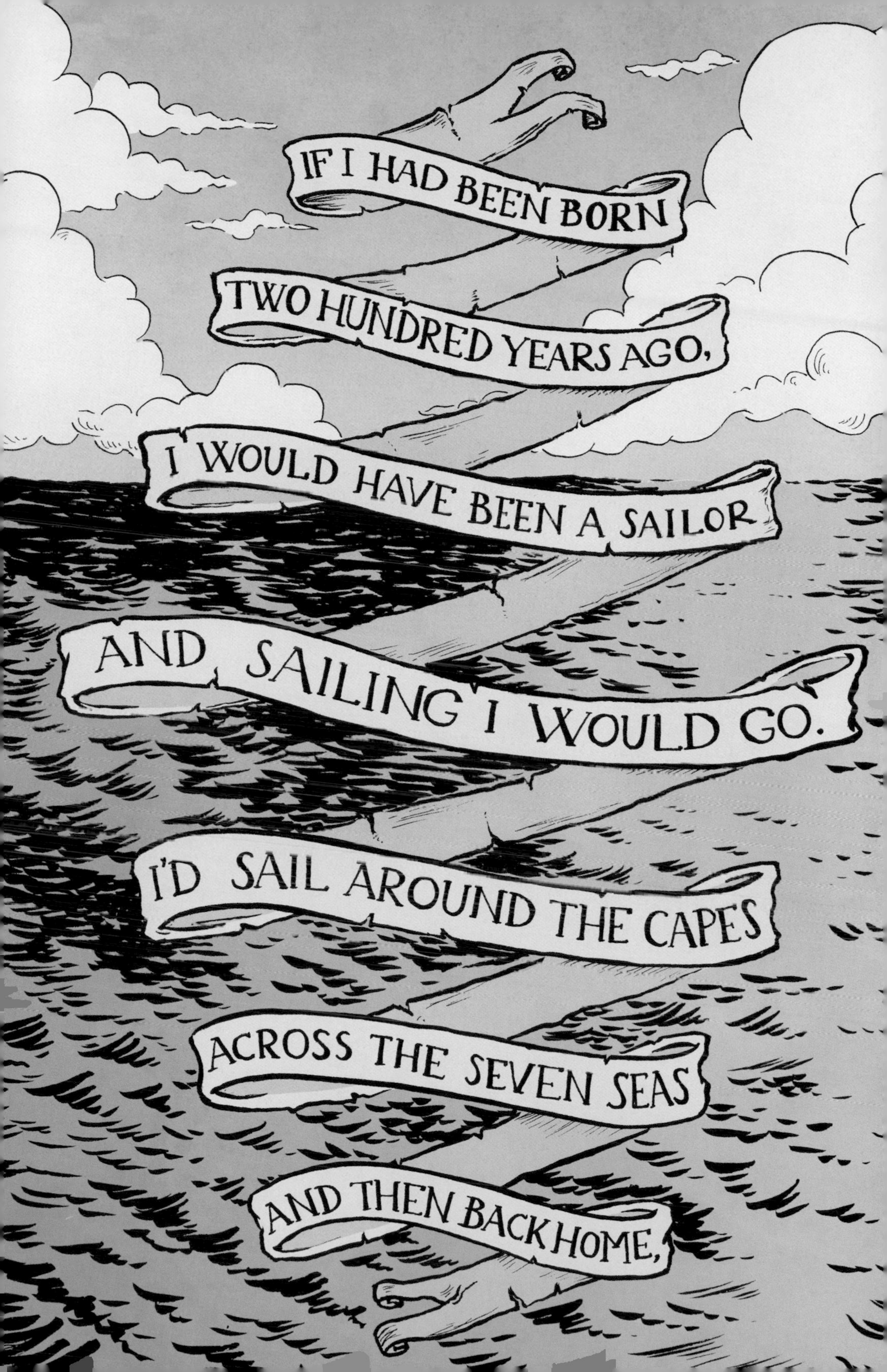
IF I HAD BEEN BORN
TWO HUNDRED YEARS AGO,
I WOULD HAVE BEEN A SAILOR
AND SAILING I WOULD GO.
I'D SAIL AROUND THE CAPES
ACROSS THE SEVEN SEAS
AND THEN BACK HOME,

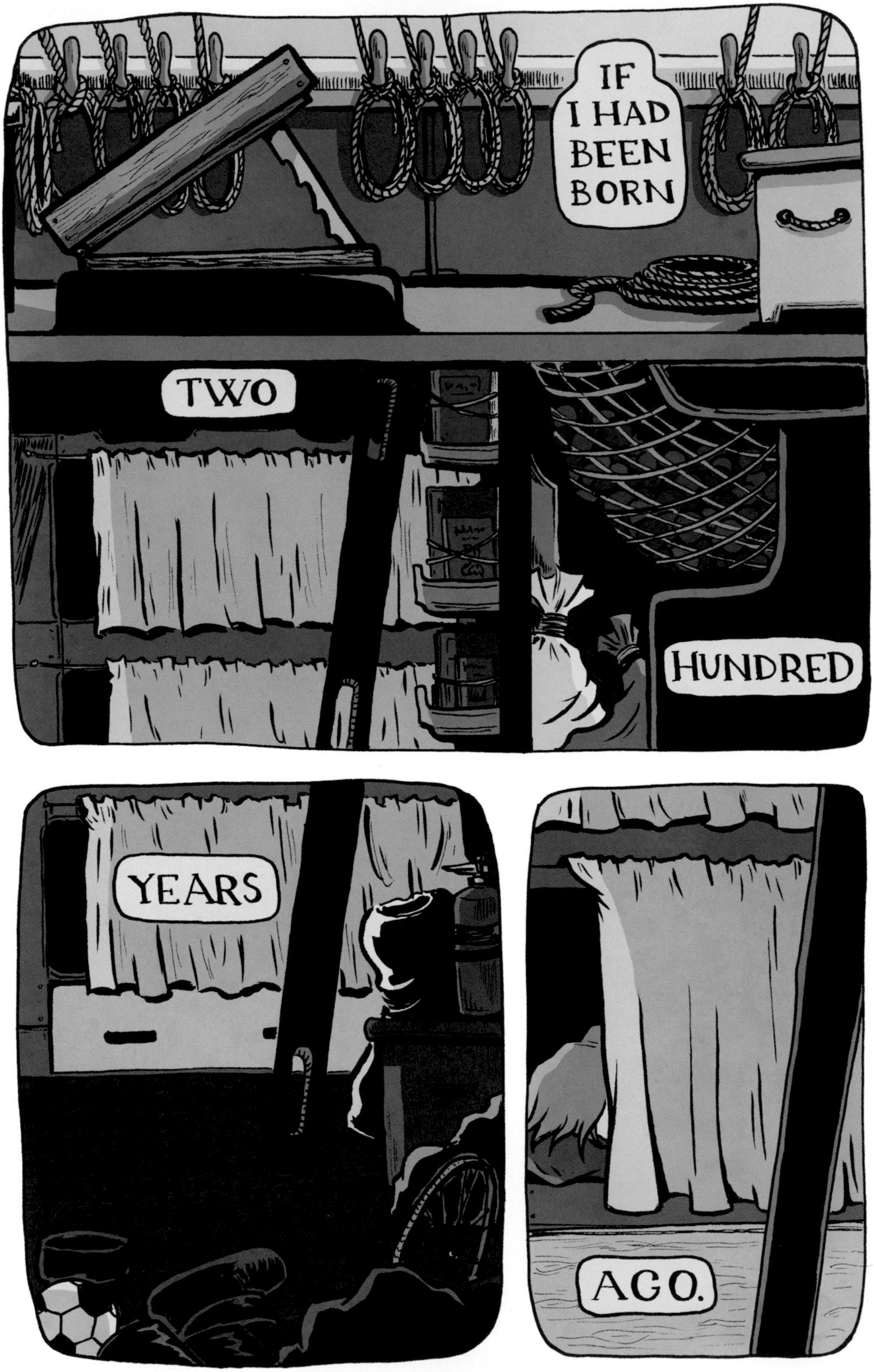
IF I HAD BEEN BORN
TWO
HUNDRED
YEARS
AGO.

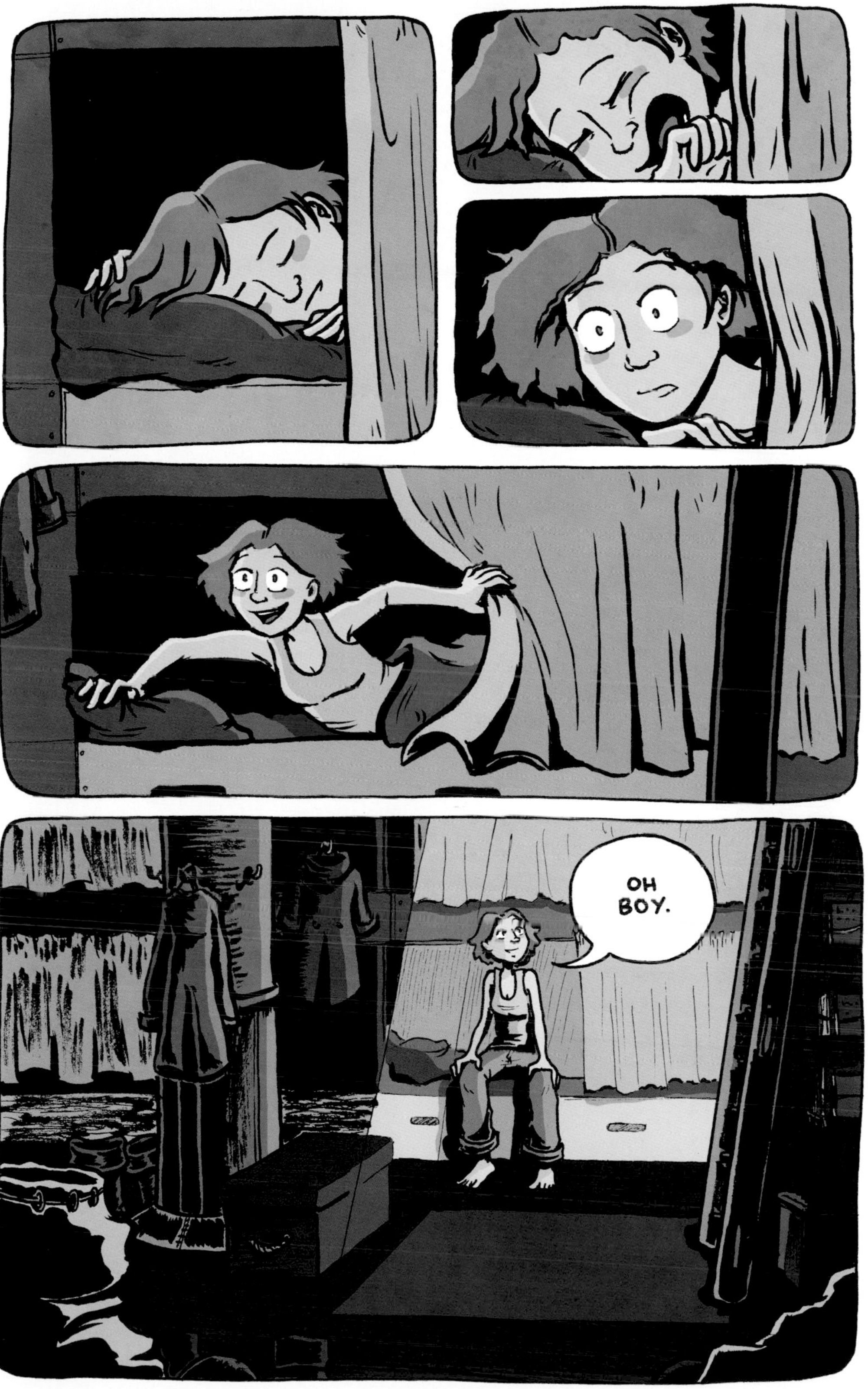
OH BOY.

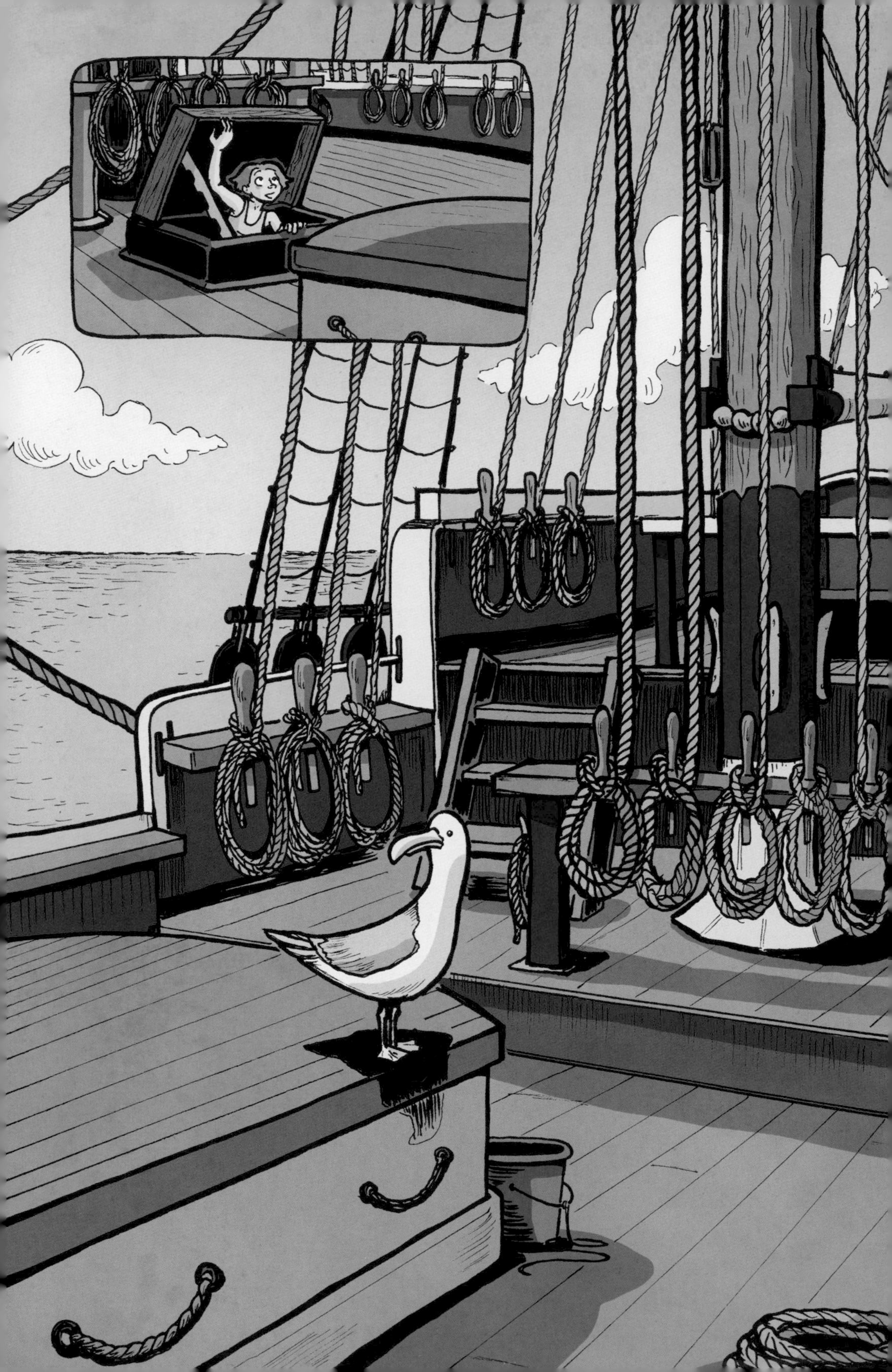

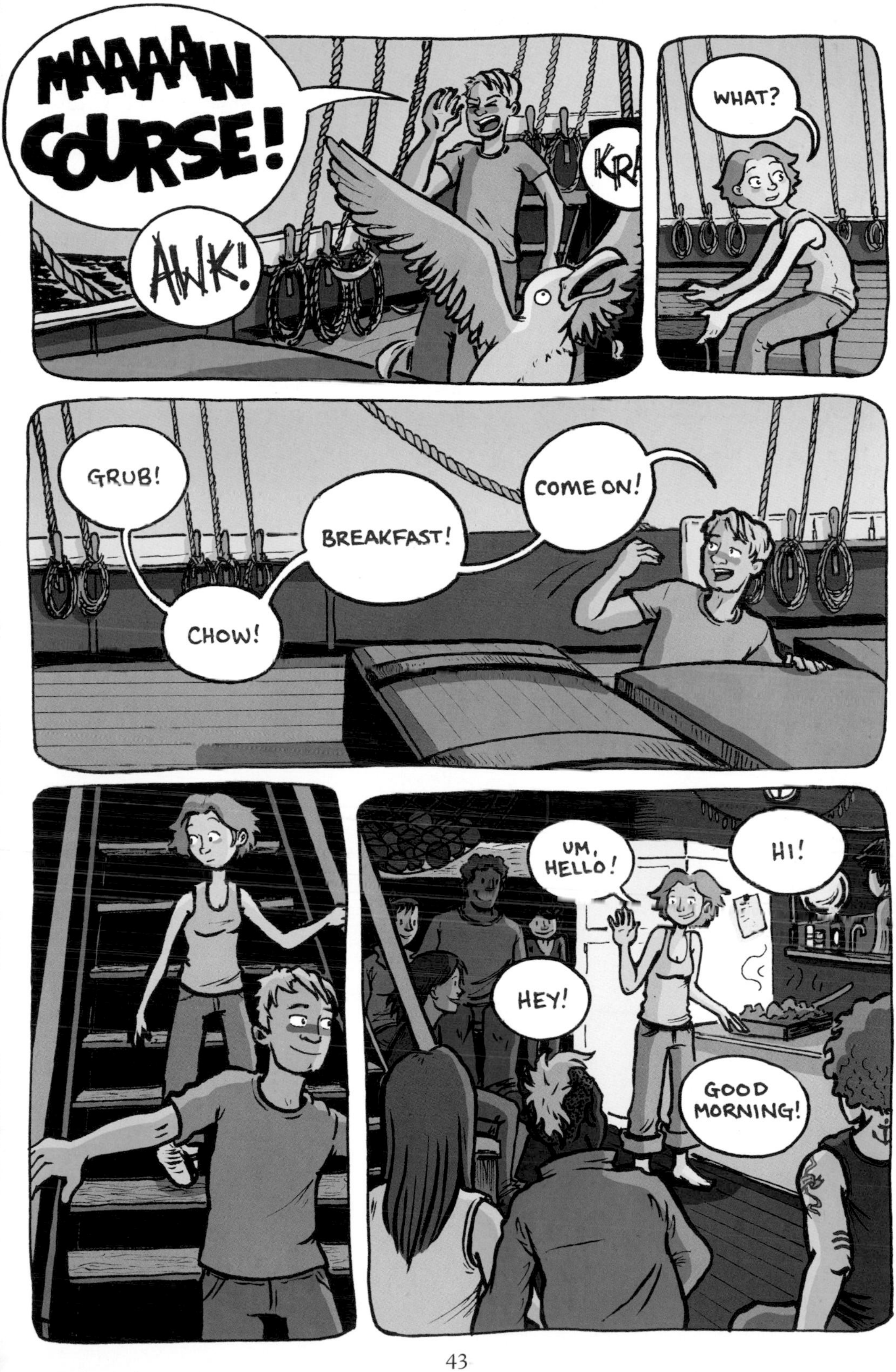
MAAAAIN COURSE!
AWK!
KRA
WHAT?
GRUB!
CHOW!
BREAKFAST!
COME ON!
UM, HELLO!
HI!
HEY!
GOOD MORNING!

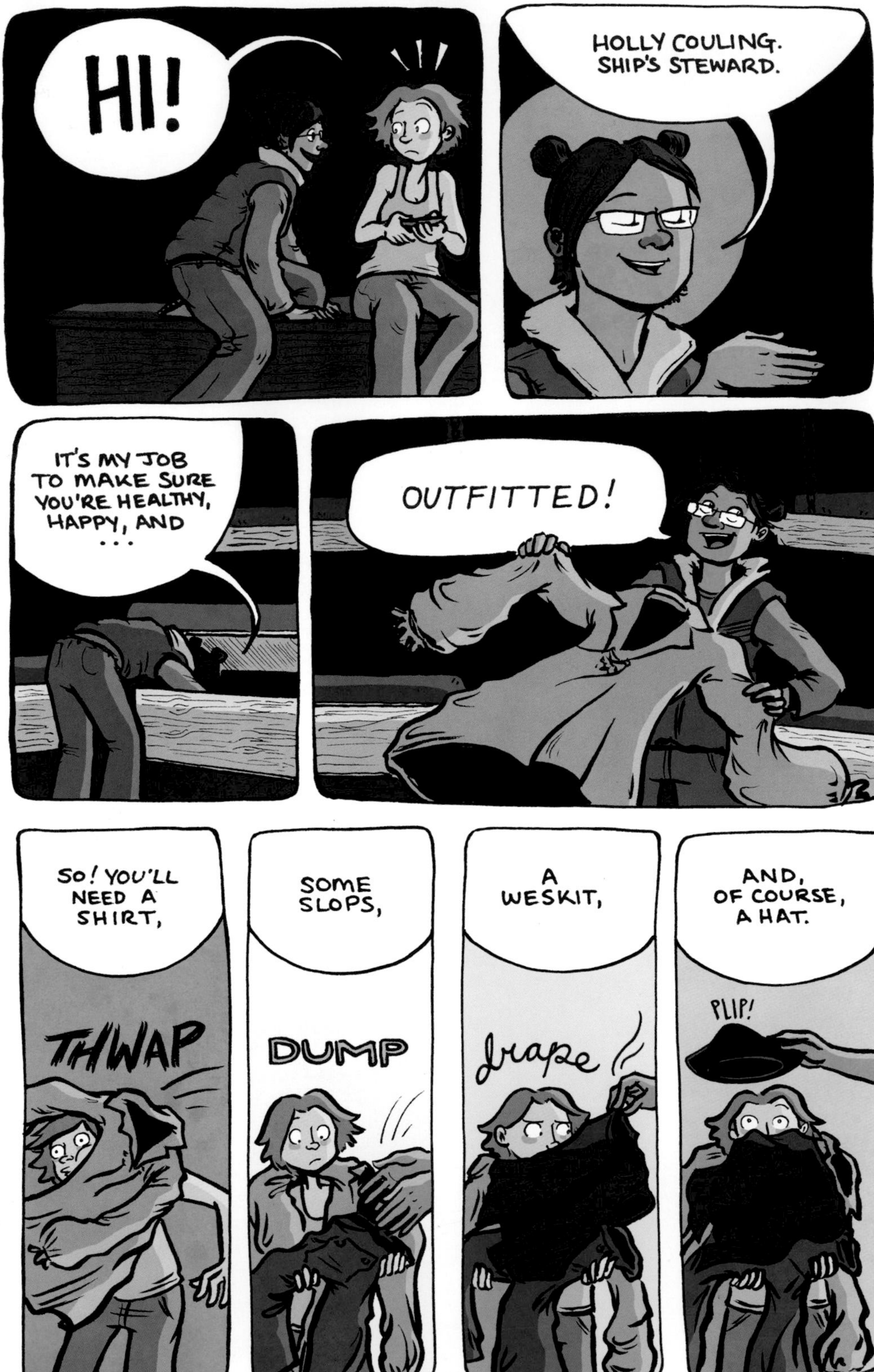
HI!
HOLLY COULING. SHIP'S STEWARD.
IT'S MY JOB TO MAKE SURE YOU'RE HEALTHY, HAPPY, AND . . .
OUTFITTED!
SO! YOU'LL NEED A SHIRT,
THWAP
SOME SLOPS,
DUMP
A WESKIT,
drape
AND, OF COURSE, A HAT.
PLIP!

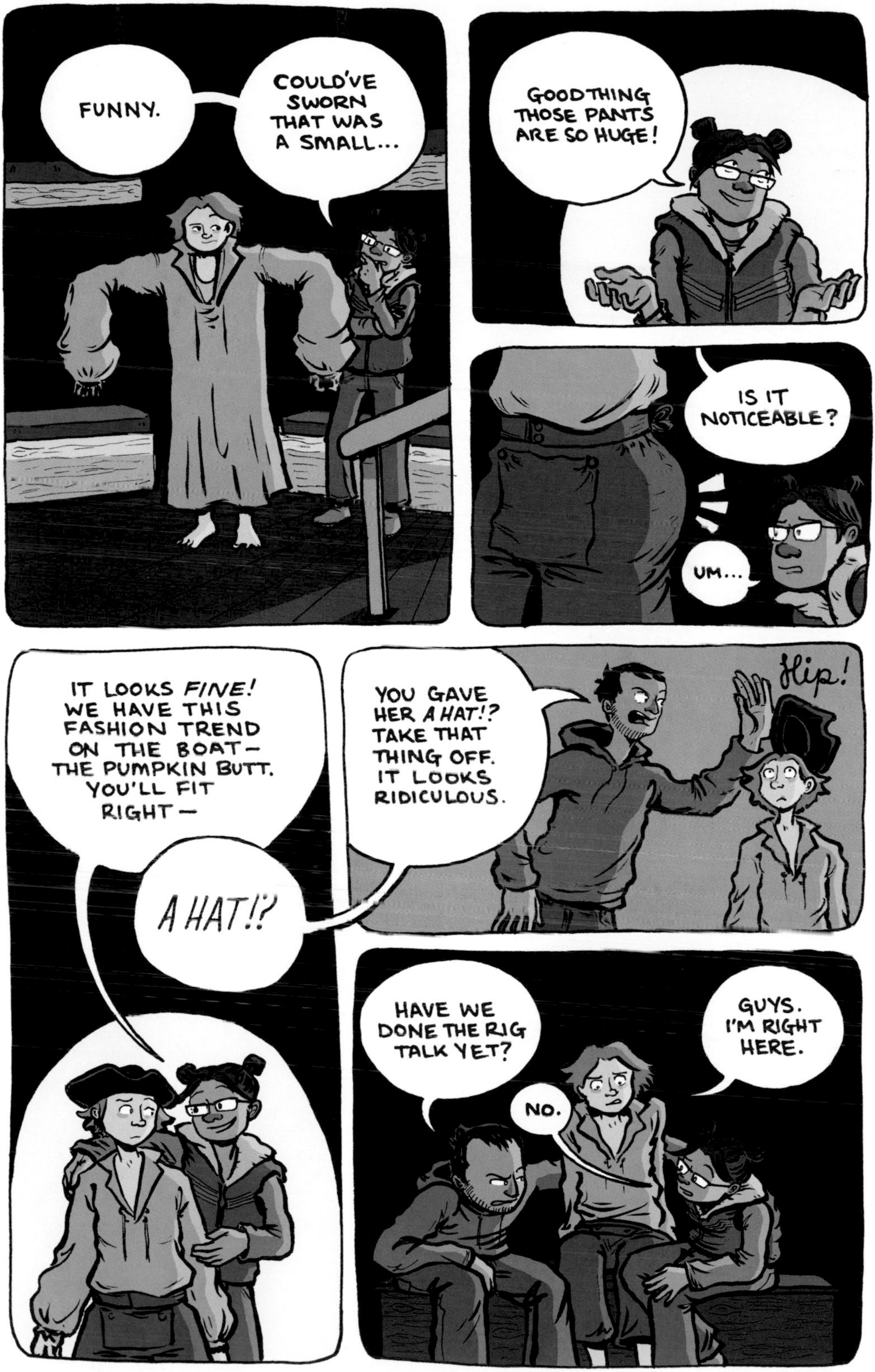
FUNNY.
COULD'VE SWORN THAT WAS A SMALL...
GOOD THING THOSE PANTS ARE SO HUGE!
IS IT NOTICEABLE?
UM...
IT LOOKS *FINE*! WE HAVE THIS FASHION TREND ON THE BOAT— THE PUMPKIN BUTT. YOU'LL FIT RIGHT—
YOU GAVE HER *A HAT!?* TAKE THAT THING OFF. IT LOOKS RIDICULOUS.
Hip!
A HAT!?
HAVE WE DONE THE RIG TALK YET?
NO.
GUYS. I'M RIGHT HERE.

SO YOU ARE.
ANY DAY NOW, ROSCOE.
RIGHT! LET'S BEGIN.
A RIG IS A SAILOR'S ETERNAL COMPANION —A UNIQUE REFLECTION OF HIS VERY *SOUL*.
NO TWO ARE ALIKE.
OBSERVE:
SHEEPSFOOT TIP PREVENTS ACCIDENTAL SHIPMATE STABBINGS WHILE WORKING ALOFT.
FANCYWORKED HANDLE TO SHOW OFF ONE'S SKILLS.
SHARP BIT FOR SLICING THROUGH TANGLED ROPE IN EMERGENCIES.

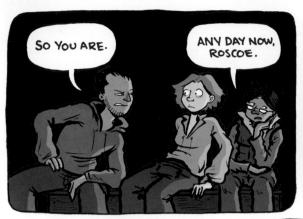

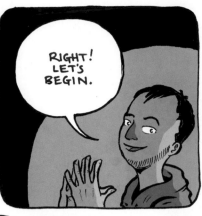

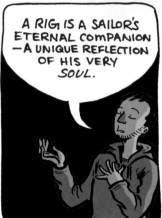

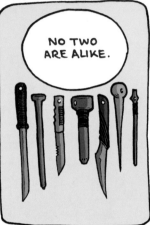

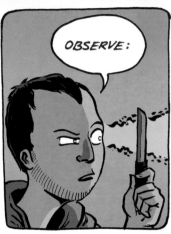

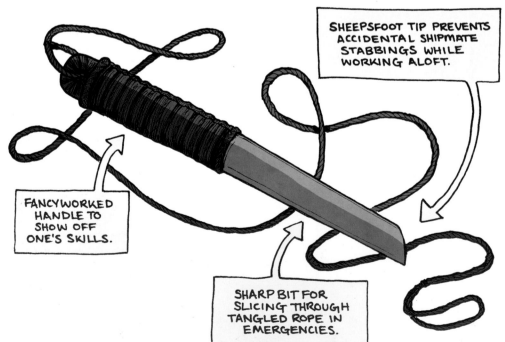

WHAT'S THE STRINGY THING?

A LANYARD.

EVERYTHING YOU TAKE ALOFT NEEDS A LANYARD.

MY TOOTHBRUSH HAS A LANYARD!

GAH!

HUH HUH HUH

THANK YOU, NICK.

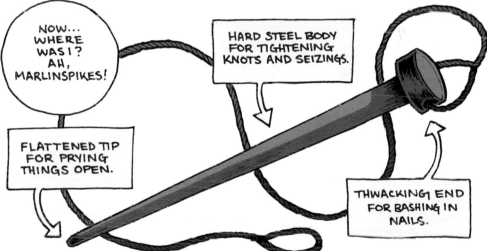

NOW... WHERE WAS I? AH, MARLINSPIKES!

HARD STEEL BODY FOR TIGHTENING KNOTS AND SEIZINGS.

FLATTENED TIP FOR PRYING THINGS OPEN.

THWACKING END FOR BASHING IN NAILS.

BUT ENOUGH ABOUT ALL THAT, FOR THE TIME HAS COME . . .

TO HAUL THINGS!

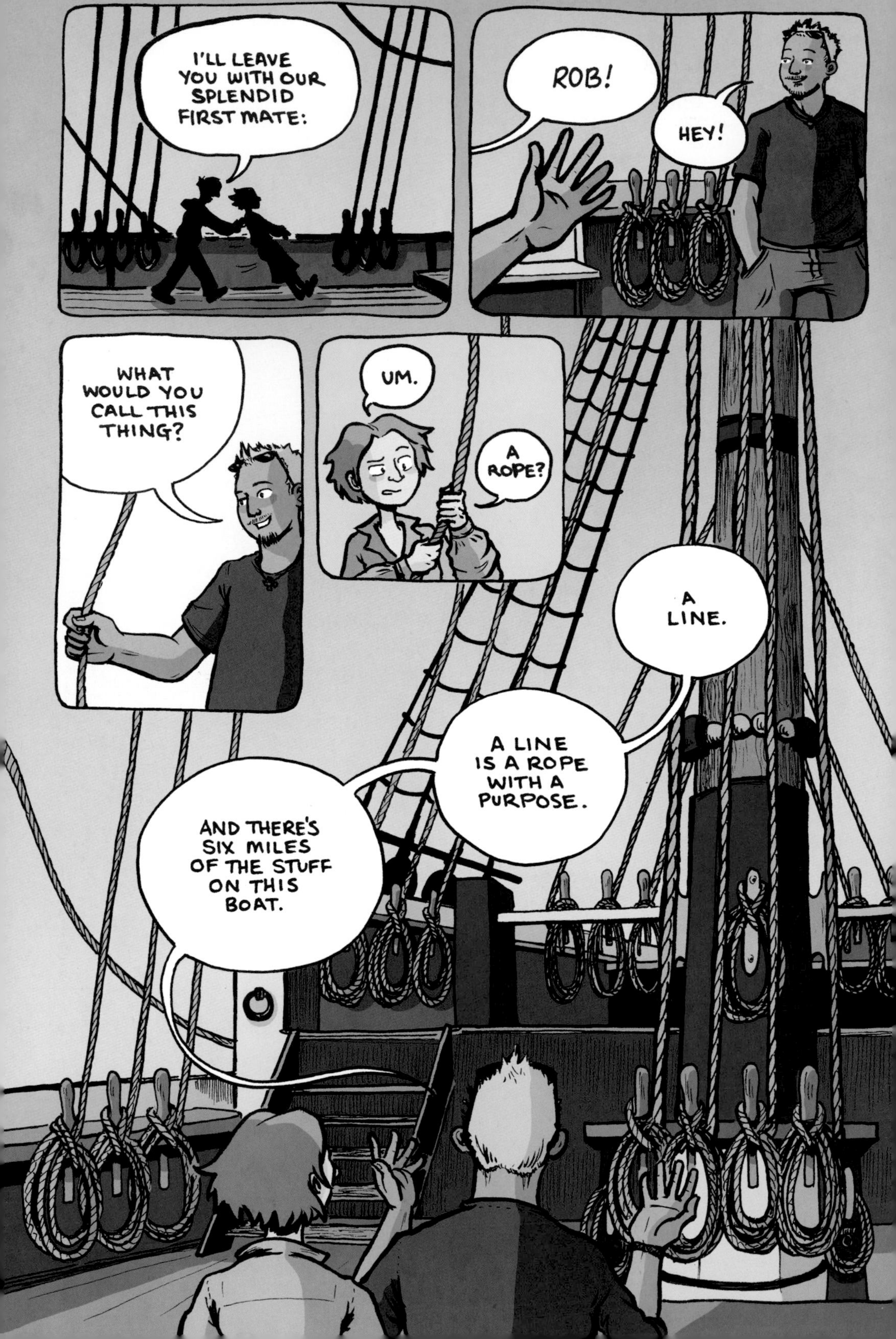
I'LL LEAVE YOU WITH OUR SPLENDID FIRST MATE:
ROB!
HEY!
WHAT WOULD YOU CALL THIS THING?
UM.
A ROPE?
A LINE.
A LINE IS A ROPE WITH A PURPOSE.
AND THERE'S SIX MILES OF THE STUFF ON THIS BOAT.

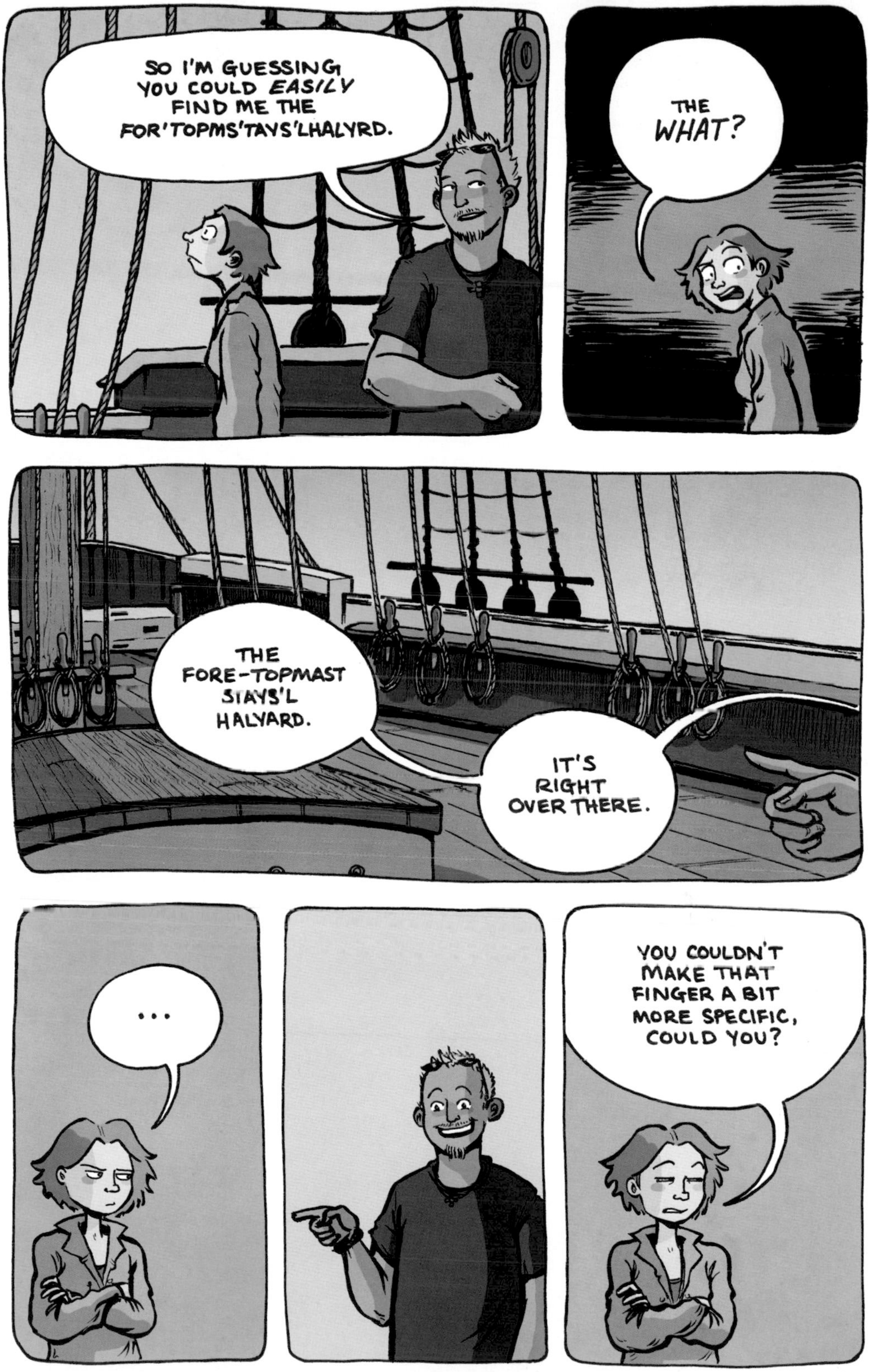
SO I'M GUESSING YOU COULD *EASILY* FIND ME THE FOR'TOPMS'TAYS'LHALYRD.
THE *WHAT?*
THE FORE-TOPMAST STAYS'L HALYARD.
IT'S RIGHT OVER THERE.
. . .
YOU COULDN'T MAKE THAT FINGER A BIT MORE SPECIFIC, COULD YOU?

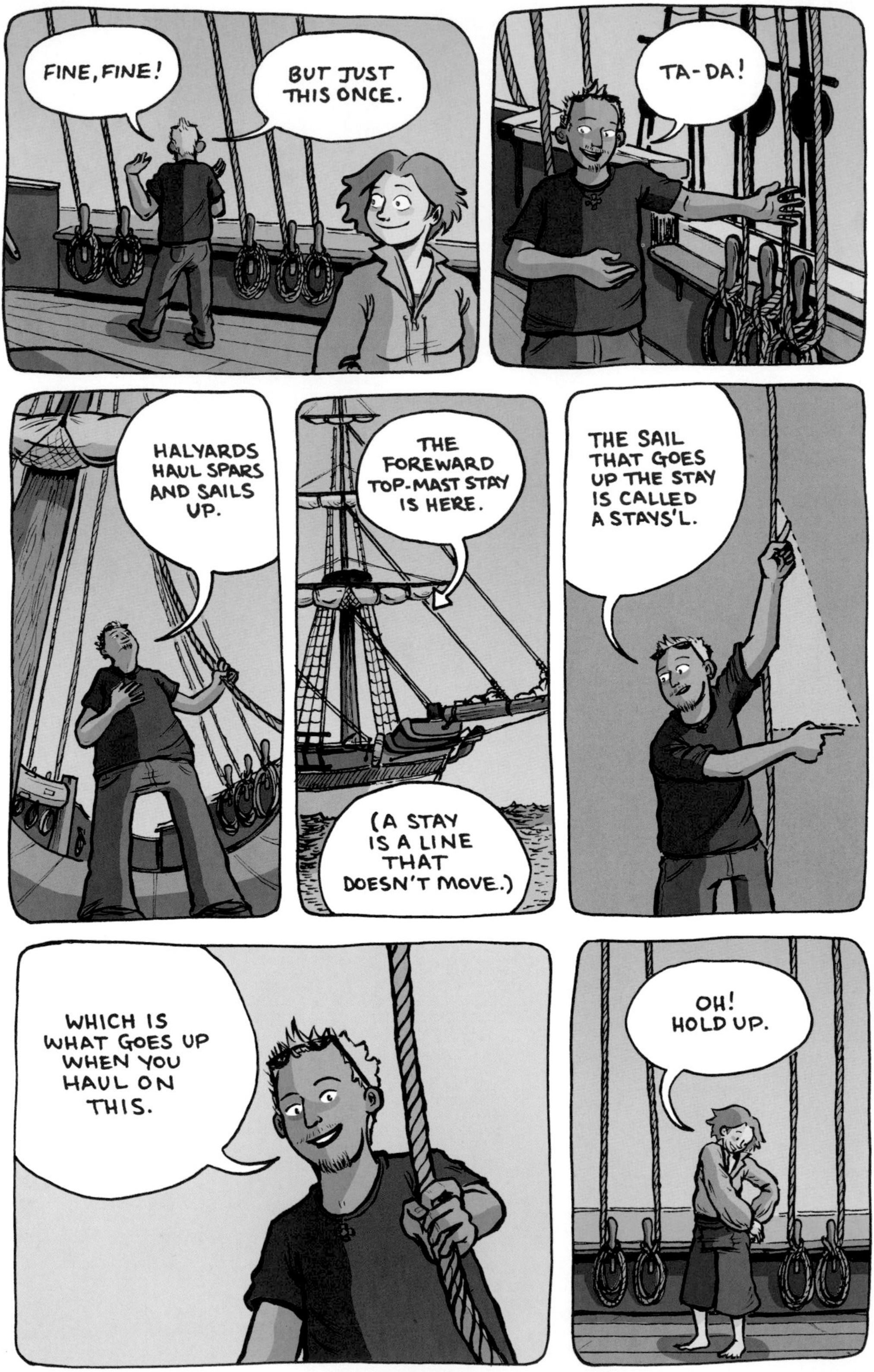
FINE, FINE!
BUT JUST THIS ONCE.
TA-DA!
HALYARDS HAUL SPARS AND SAILS UP.
THE FOREWARD TOP-MAST STAY IS HERE.
(A STAY IS A LINE THAT DOESN'T MOVE.)
THE SAIL THAT GOES UP THE STAY IS CALLED A STAYS'L.
WHICH IS WHAT GOES UP WHEN YOU HAUL ON THIS.
OH! HOLD UP.

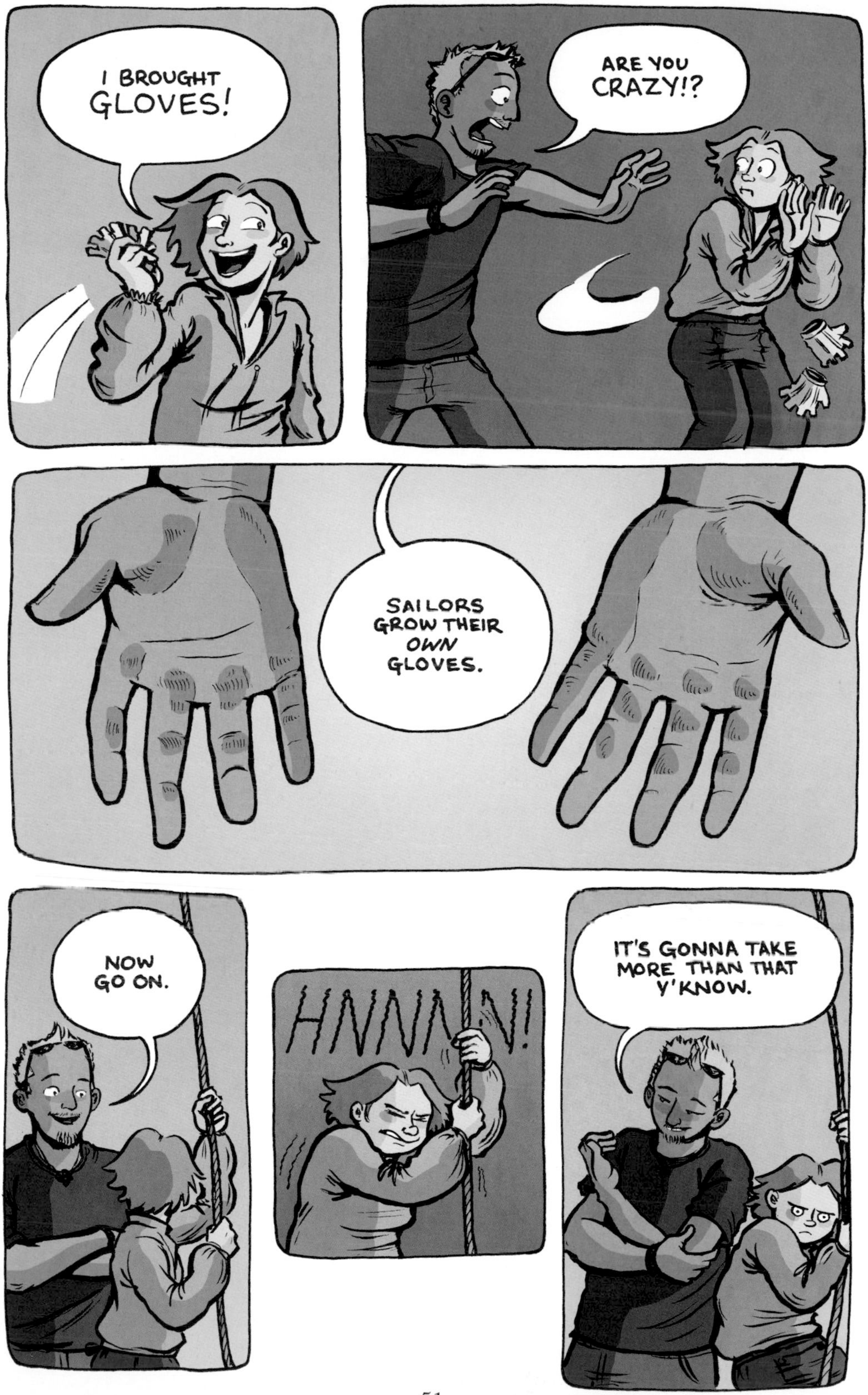
I BROUGHT GLOVES!
ARE YOU CRAZY!?
SAILORS GROW THEIR OWN GLOVES.
NOW GO ON.
HNNNNN!
IT'S GONNA TAKE MORE THAN THAT Y'KNOW.

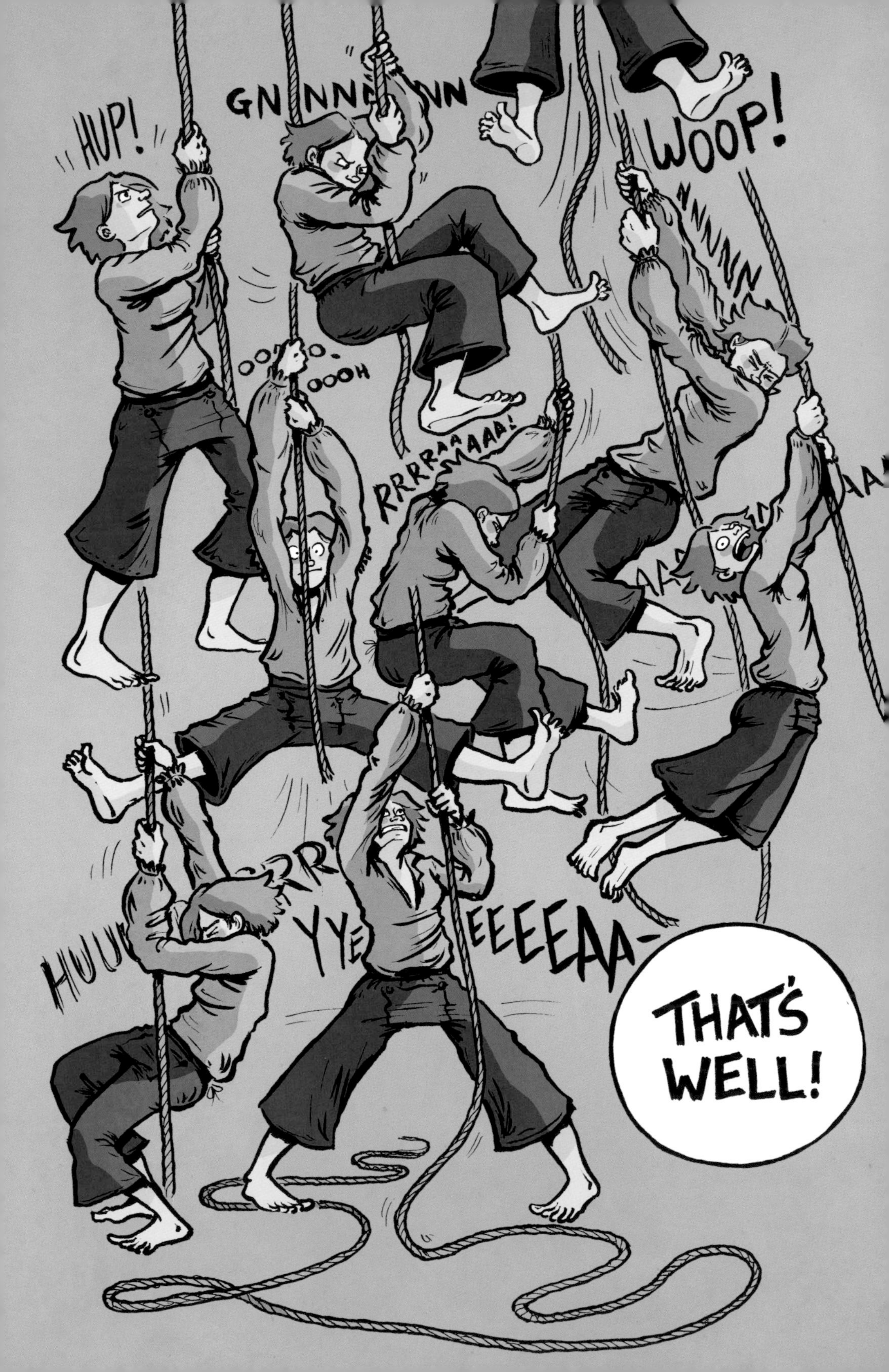
HUP!
GNNNNNNN
WOOP!
NNNNN
OOOO. OOOH
RRRRAAAAA!
HUU
RR
YYEEEEEAA-
THAT'S WELL!

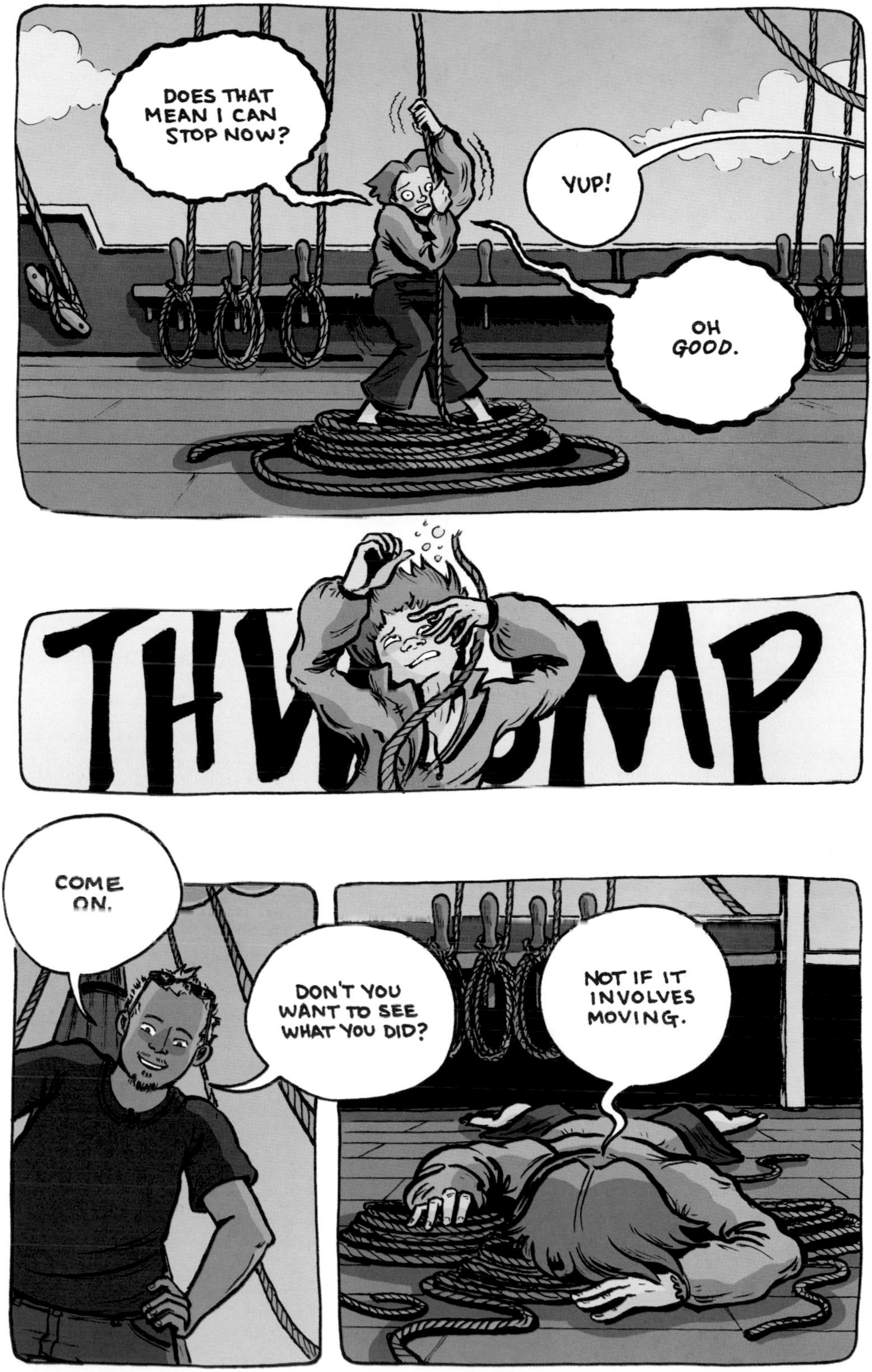
DOES THAT MEAN I CAN STOP NOW?
YUP!
OH GOOD.
THWUMP
COME ON.
DON'T YOU WANT TO SEE WHAT YOU DID?
NOT IF IT INVOLVES MOVING.

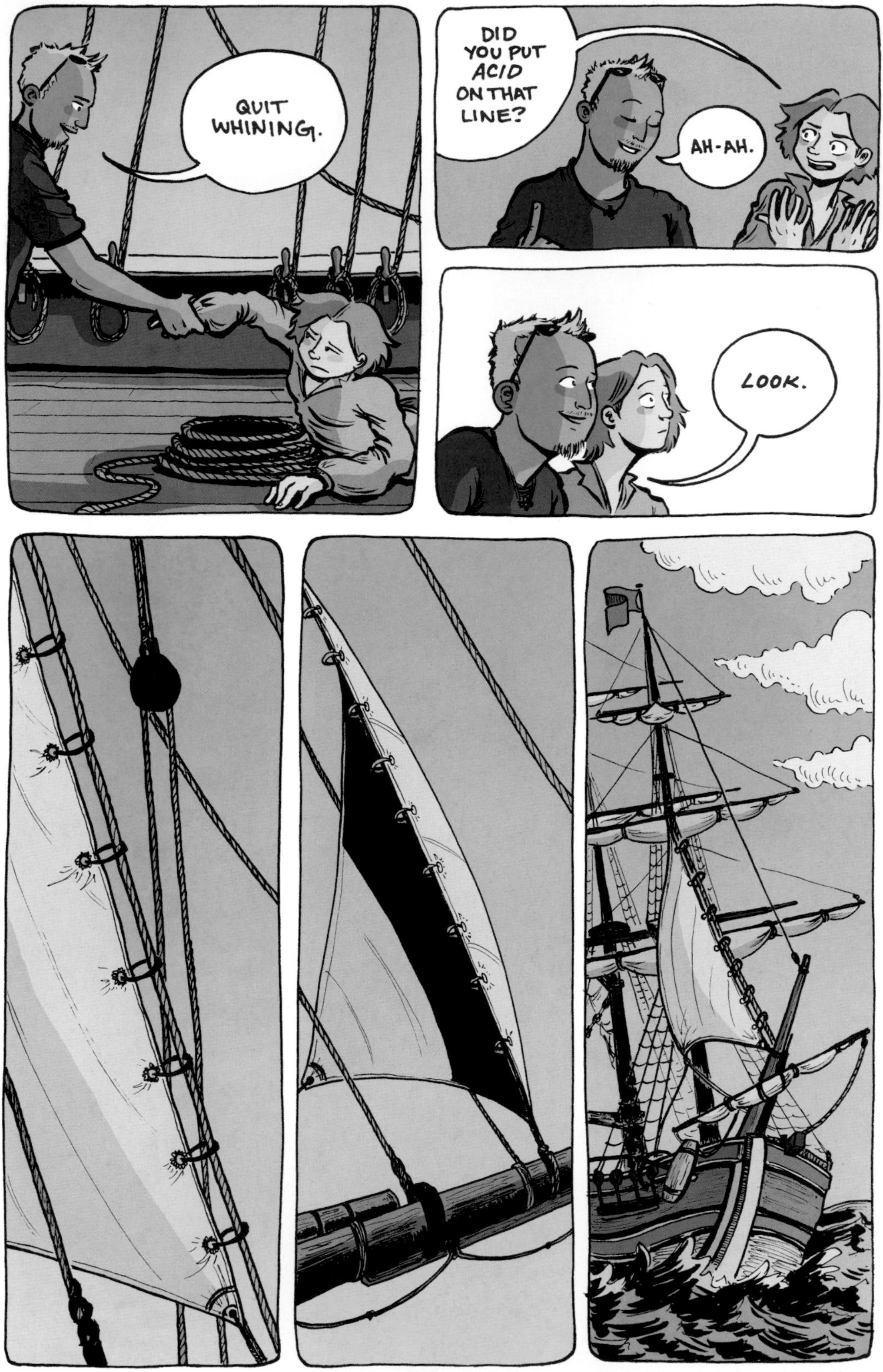
QUIT WHINING.
DID YOU PUT ACID ON THAT LINE?
AH-AH.
LOOK.

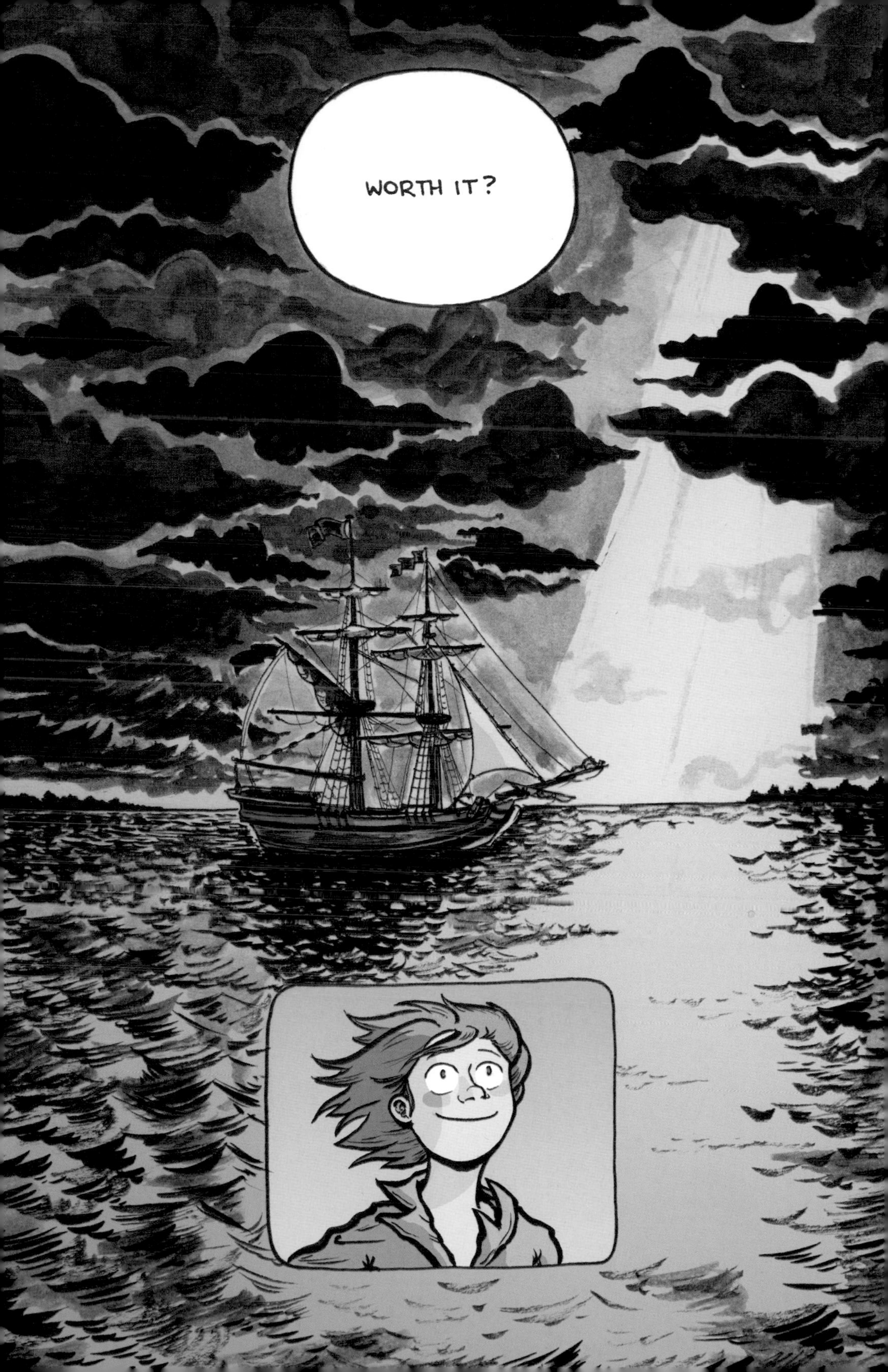
WORTH IT?

YEAH.

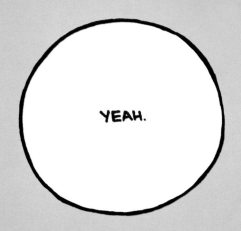

HARD TACK

THE WORLD'S OLDEST PIECE
OF HARD TACK IS KEPT
AT A DANISH MARITIME
MUSEUM IN KRONBORG CASTLE.

THE BISCUIT DATES
FROM 1852.

HARD TACK IS A STAPLE
OF THE NAUTICAL DIET.
IT IS ALSO
COMPLETELY DISGUSTING.

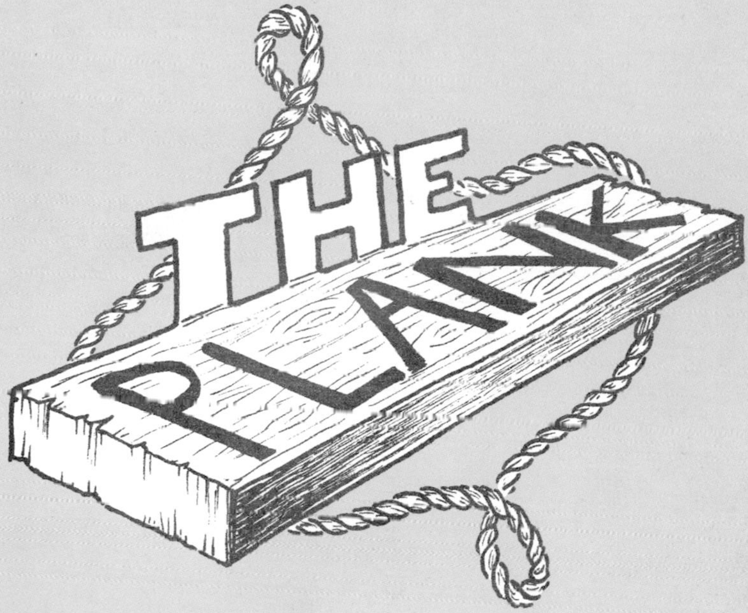
THE
PLANK

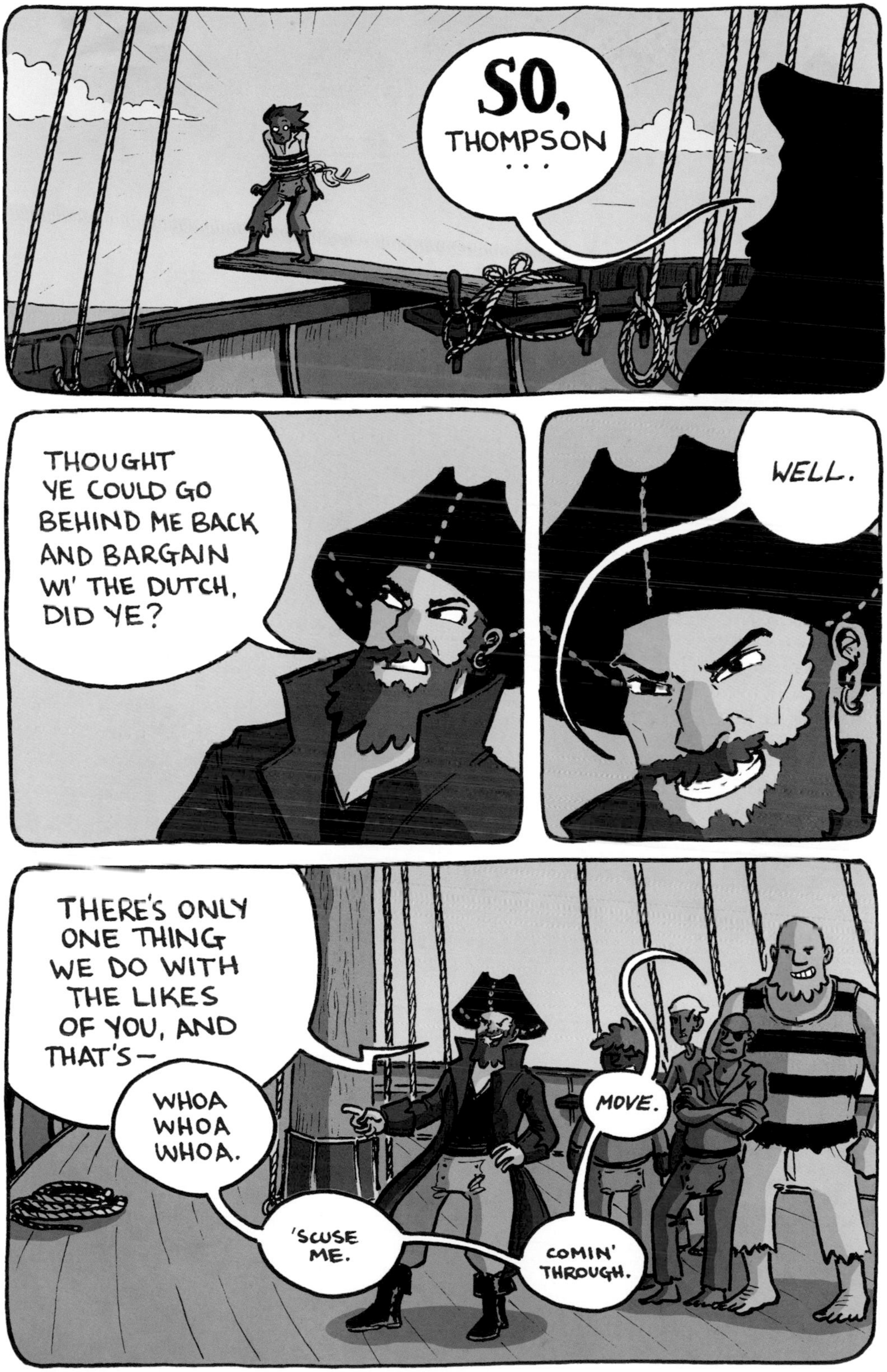
SO, THOMPSON ...
THOUGHT YE COULD GO BEHIND ME BACK AND BARGAIN WI' THE DUTCH, DID YE?
WELL.
THERE'S ONLY ONE THING WE DO WITH THE LIKES OF YOU, AND THAT'S—
WHOA WHOA WHOA.
'SCUSE ME.
COMIN' THROUGH.
MOVE.

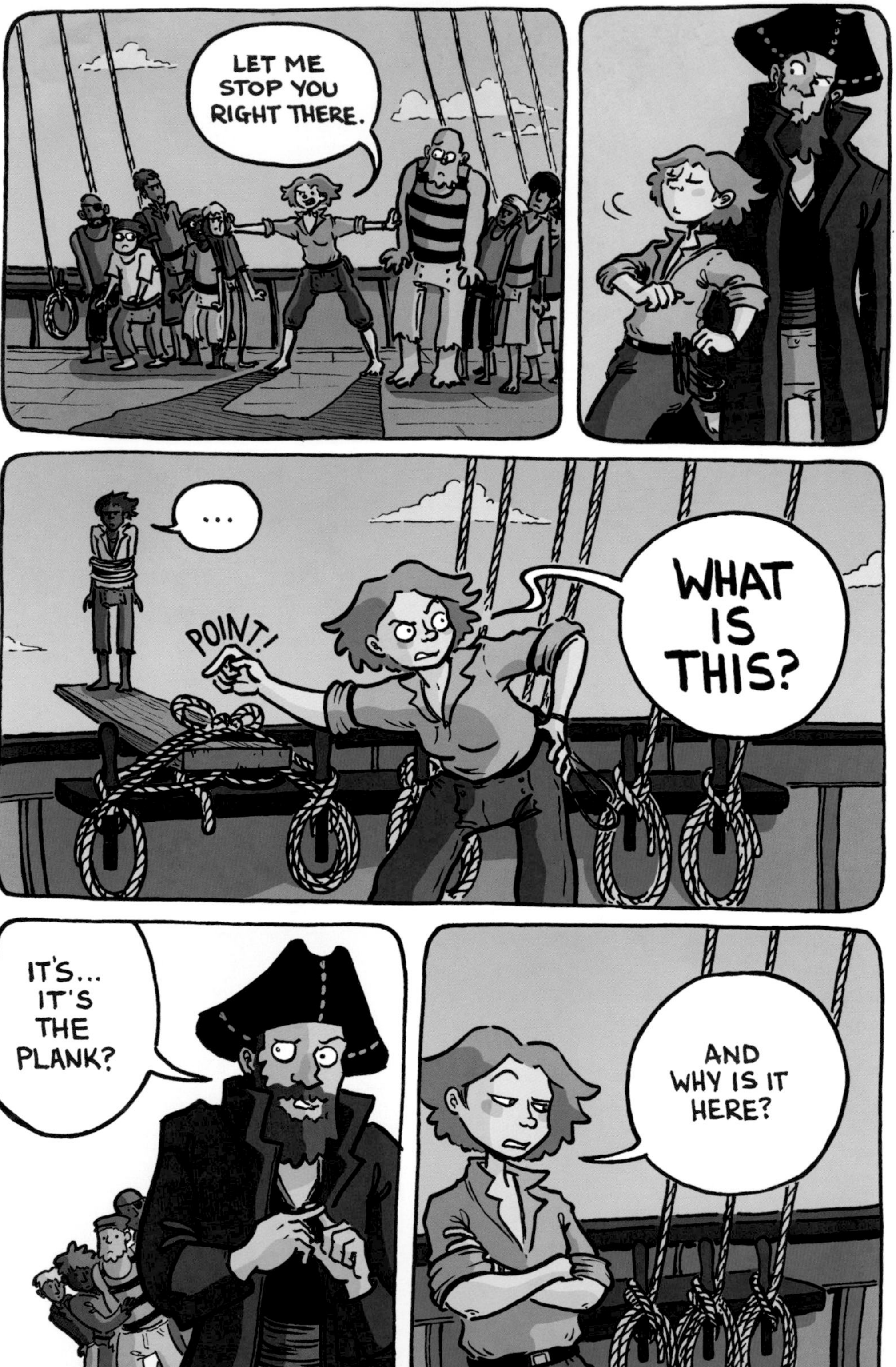
LET ME STOP YOU RIGHT THERE.
...
POINT!
WHAT IS THIS?
IT'S... IT'S THE PLANK?
AND WHY IS IT HERE?

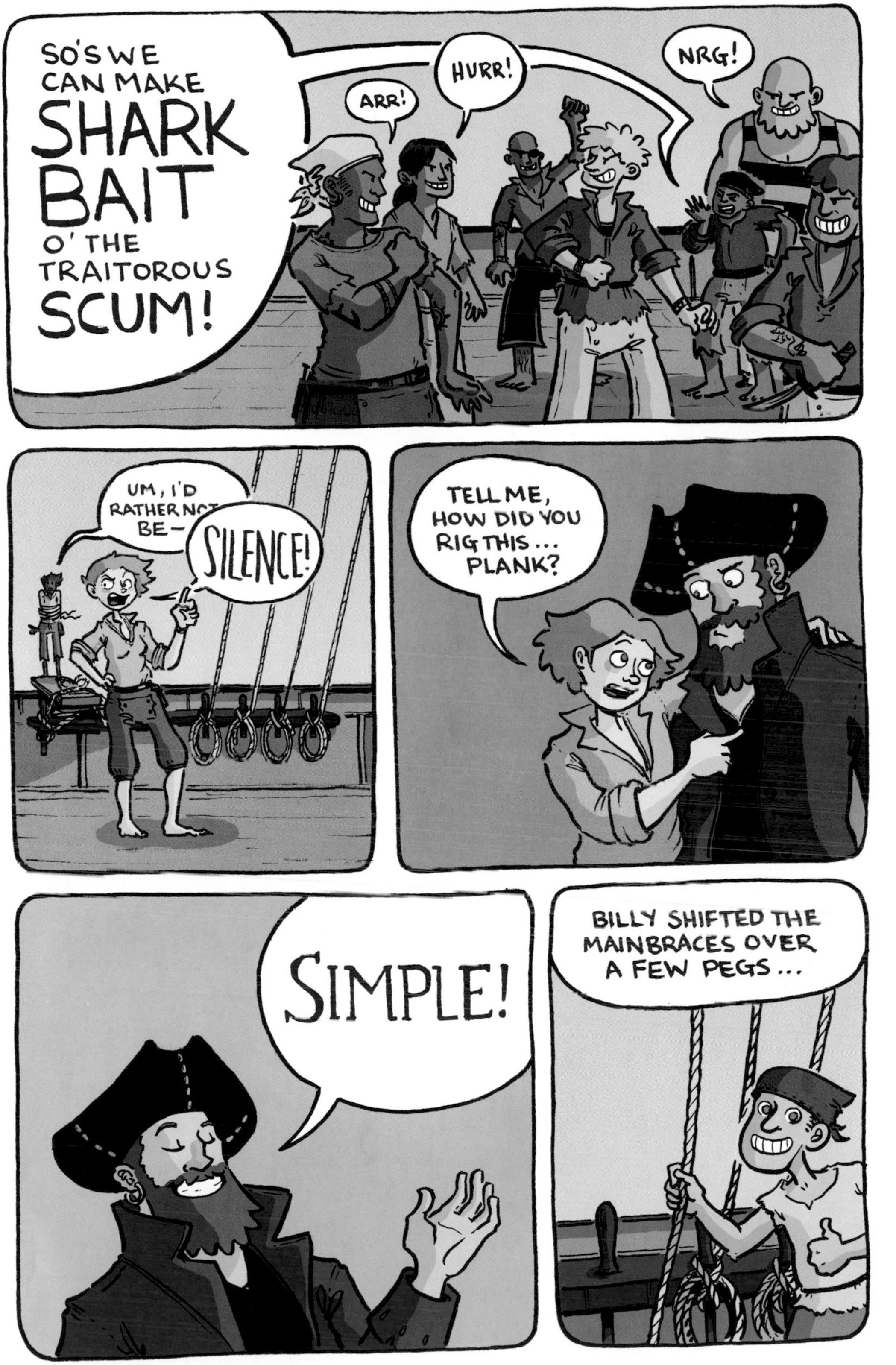
SO'S WE CAN MAKE SHARK BAIT O' THE TRAITOROUS SCUM!
ARR!
HURR!
NRG!
UM, I'D RATHER NOT BE—
SILENCE!
TELL ME, HOW DID YOU RIG THIS... PLANK?
SIMPLE!
BILLY SHIFTED THE MAINBRACES OVER A FEW PEGS...

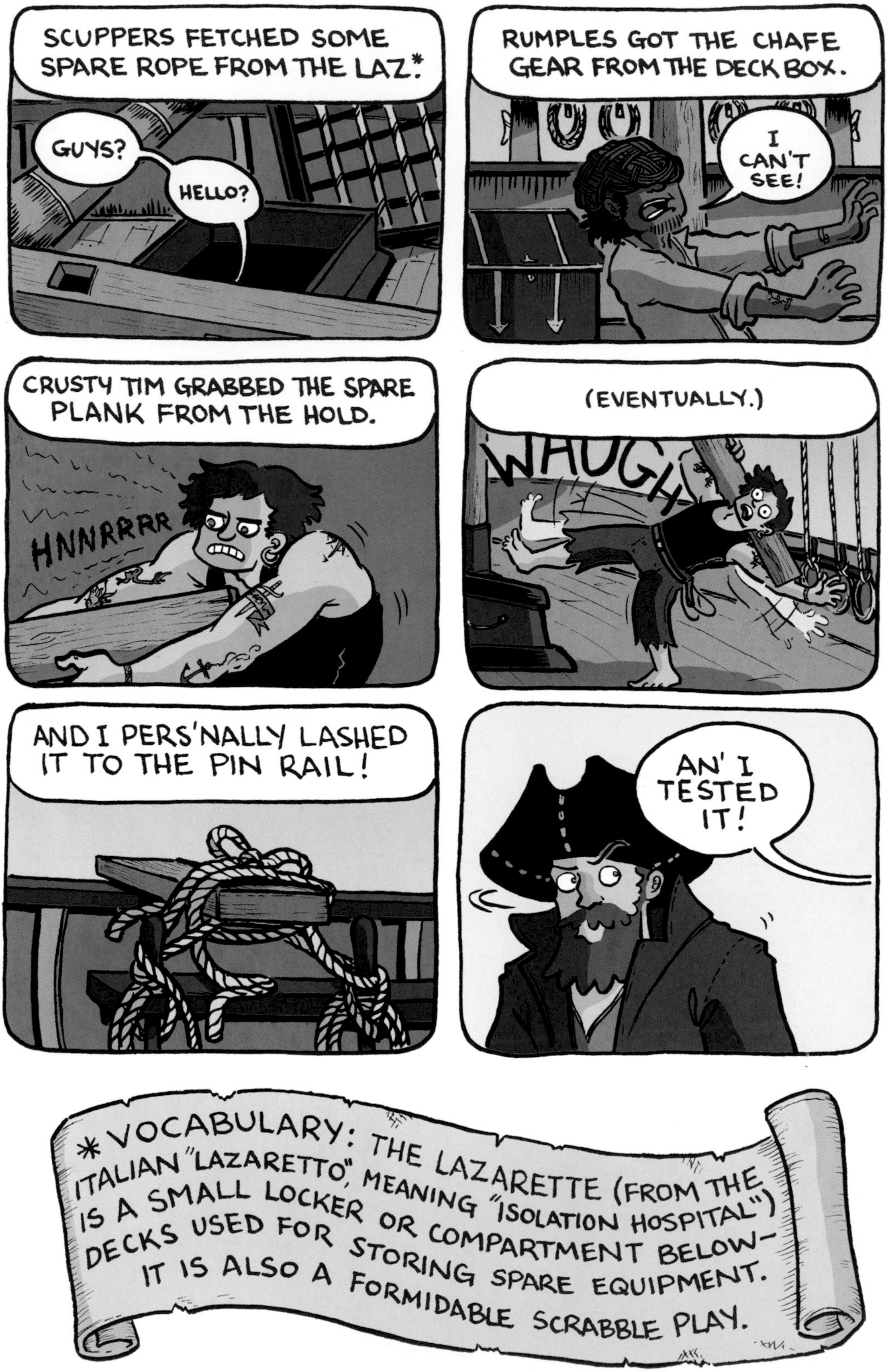
SCUPPERS FETCHED SOME SPARE ROPE FROM THE LAZ.*
GUYS?
HELLO?
RUMPLES GOT THE CHAFE GEAR FROM THE DECK BOX.
I CAN'T SEE!
CRUSTY TIM GRABBED THE SPARE PLANK FROM THE HOLD.
HNNRRRR
(EVENTUALLY.)
WAUGH
AND I PERS'NALLY LASHED IT TO THE PIN RAIL!
AN' I TESTED IT!
* VOCABULARY: THE LAZARETTE (FROM THE ITALIAN "LAZARETTO", MEANING "ISOLATION HOSPITAL") IS A SMALL LOCKER OR COMPARTMENT BELOW DECKS USED FOR STORING SPARE EQUIPMENT. IT IS ALSO A FORMIDABLE SCRABBLE PLAY.

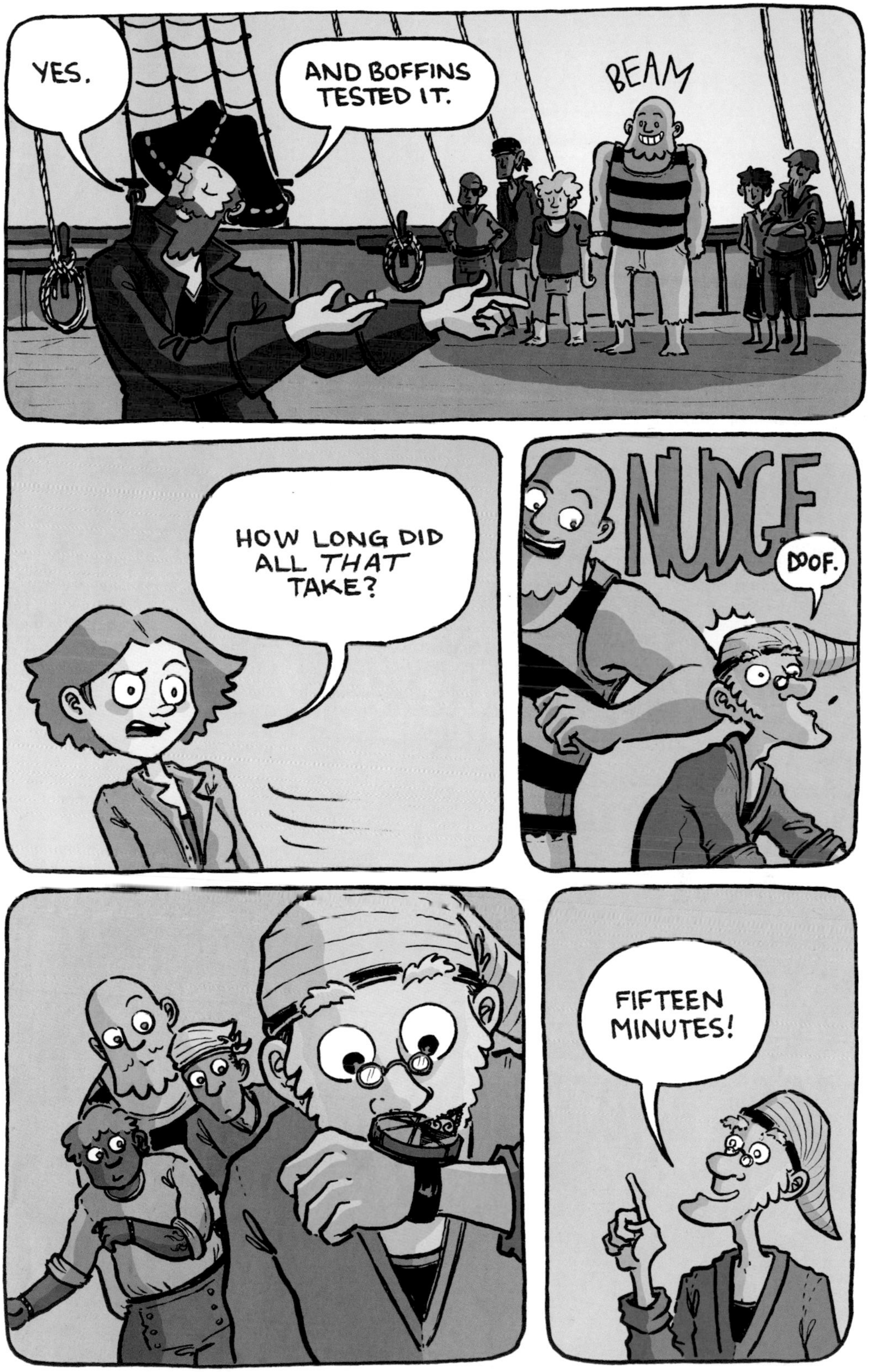
YES.
AND BOFFINS TESTED IT.
BEAM
HOW LONG DID ALL *THAT* TAKE?
NUDGE
DOOF.
FIFTEEN MINUTES!

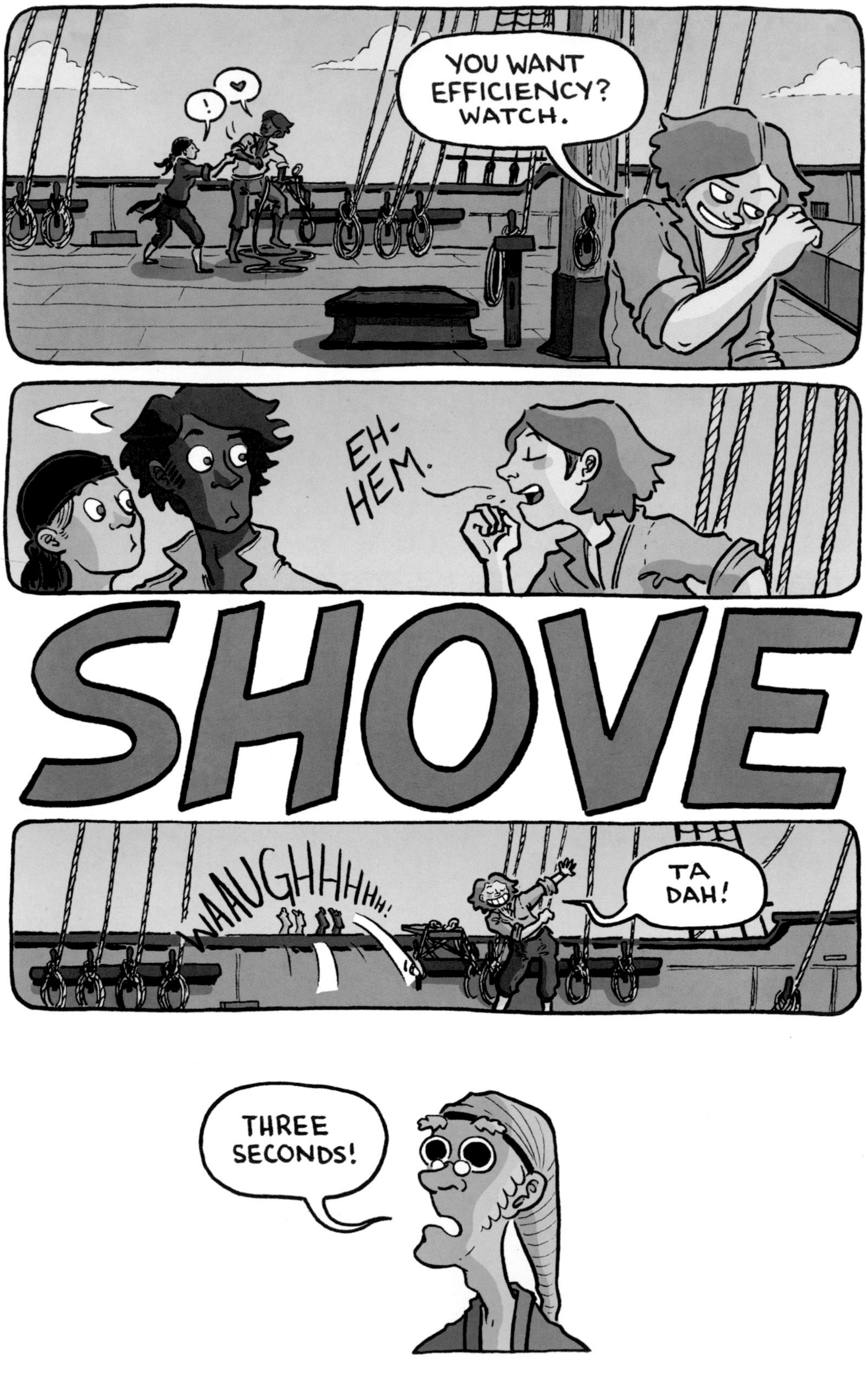
!
YOU WANT EFFICIENCY? WATCH.
EH-HEM.
SHOVE
WAAUGHHHHH!
TA DAH!
THREE SECONDS!

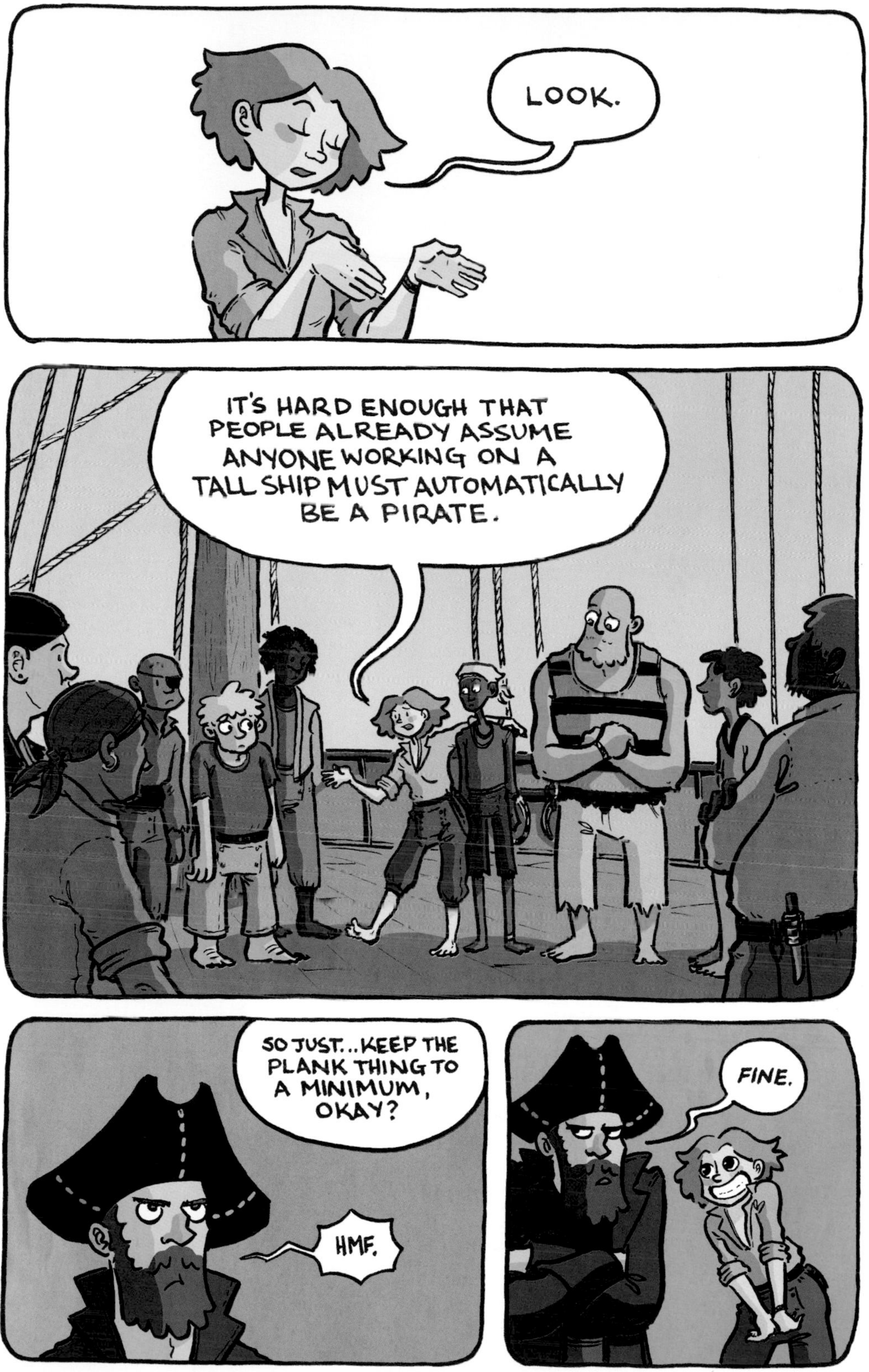
LOOK.
IT'S HARD ENOUGH THAT PEOPLE ALREADY ASSUME ANYONE WORKING ON A TALL SHIP MUST AUTOMATICALLY BE A PIRATE.
SO JUST...KEEP THE PLANK THING TO A MINIMUM, OKAY?
HMF.
FINE.

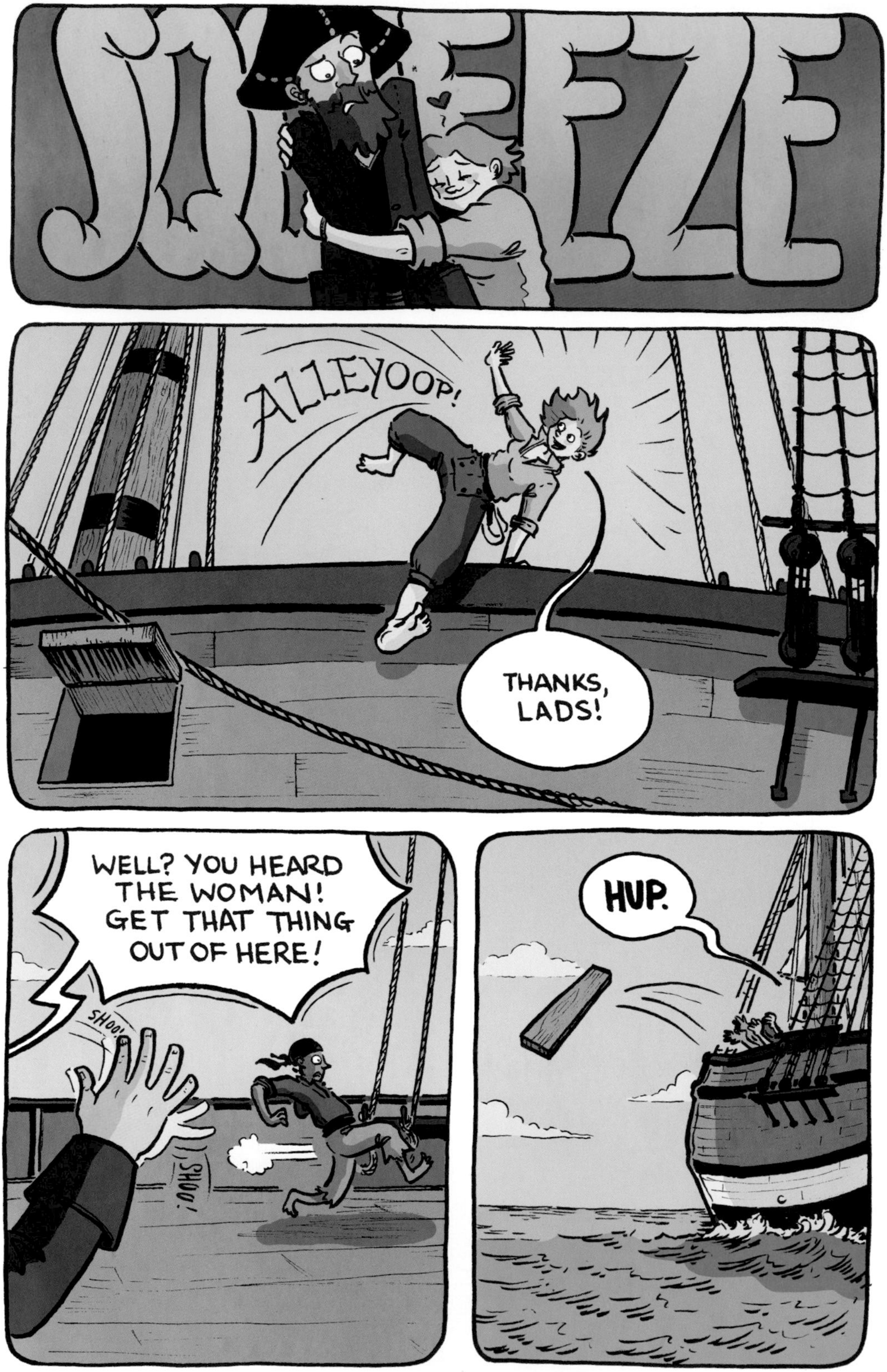
SQUEEZE
ALLEYOOP!
THANKS, LADS!
WELL? YOU HEARD THE WOMAN! GET THAT THING OUT OF HERE!
SHOO!
SHOO!
HUP.

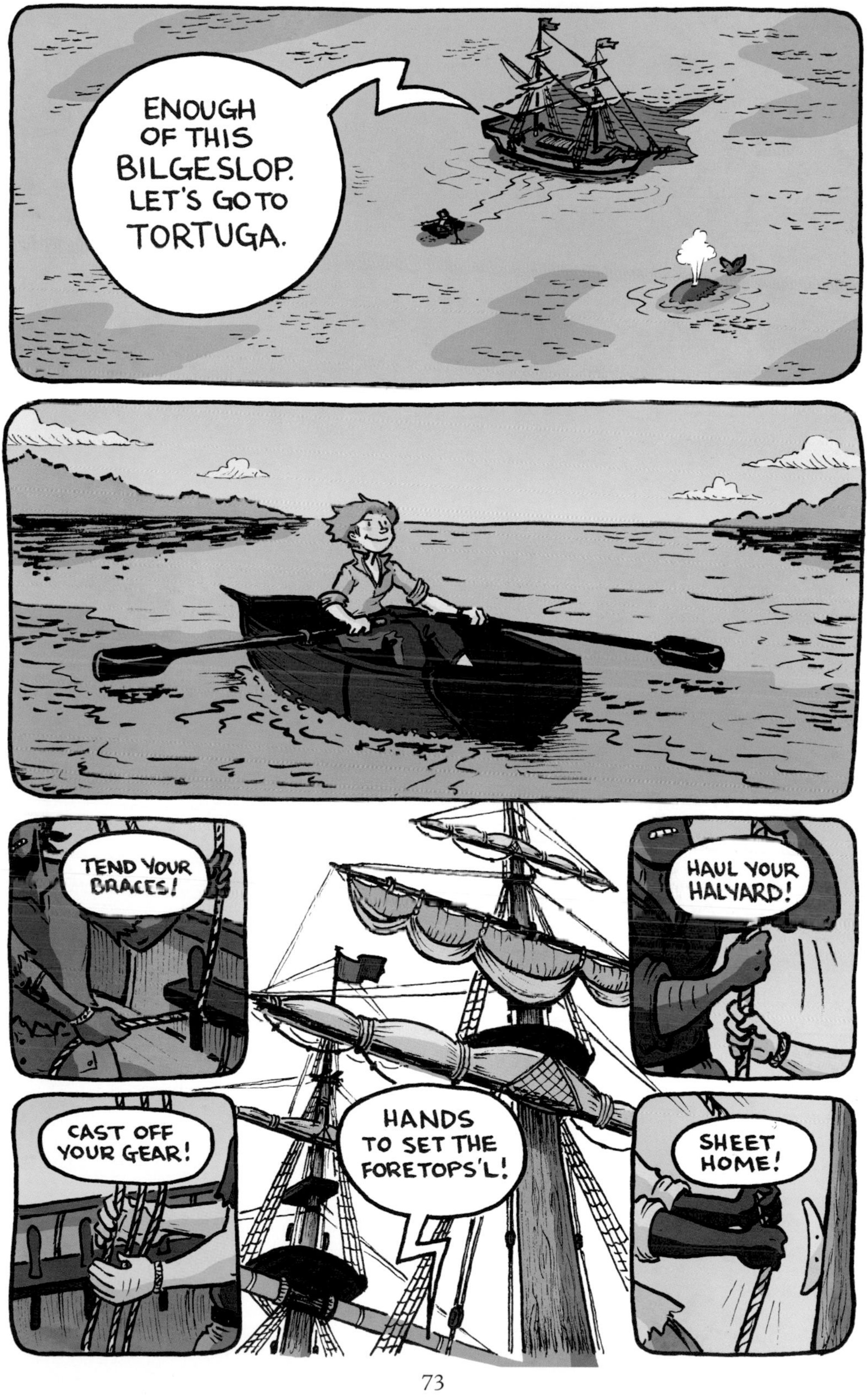
ENOUGH OF THIS BILGESLOP. LET'S GO TO TORTUGA.
TEND YOUR BRACES!
HAUL YOUR HALYARD!
CAST OFF YOUR GEAR!
HANDS TO SET THE FORETOPS'L!
SHEET HOME!

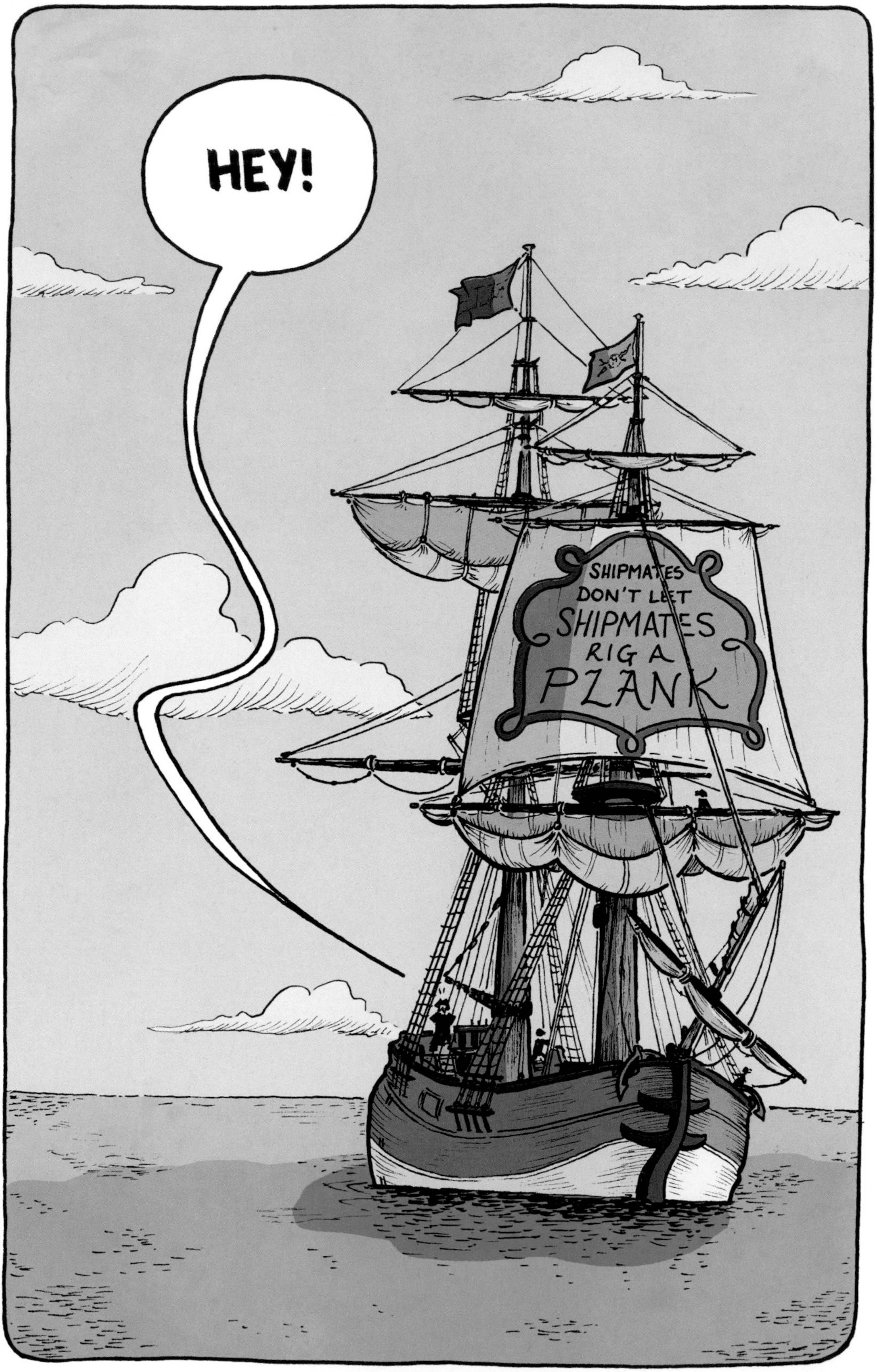
HEY!
SHIPMATES DON'T LET SHIPMATES RIG A PLANK

Pacific Passages

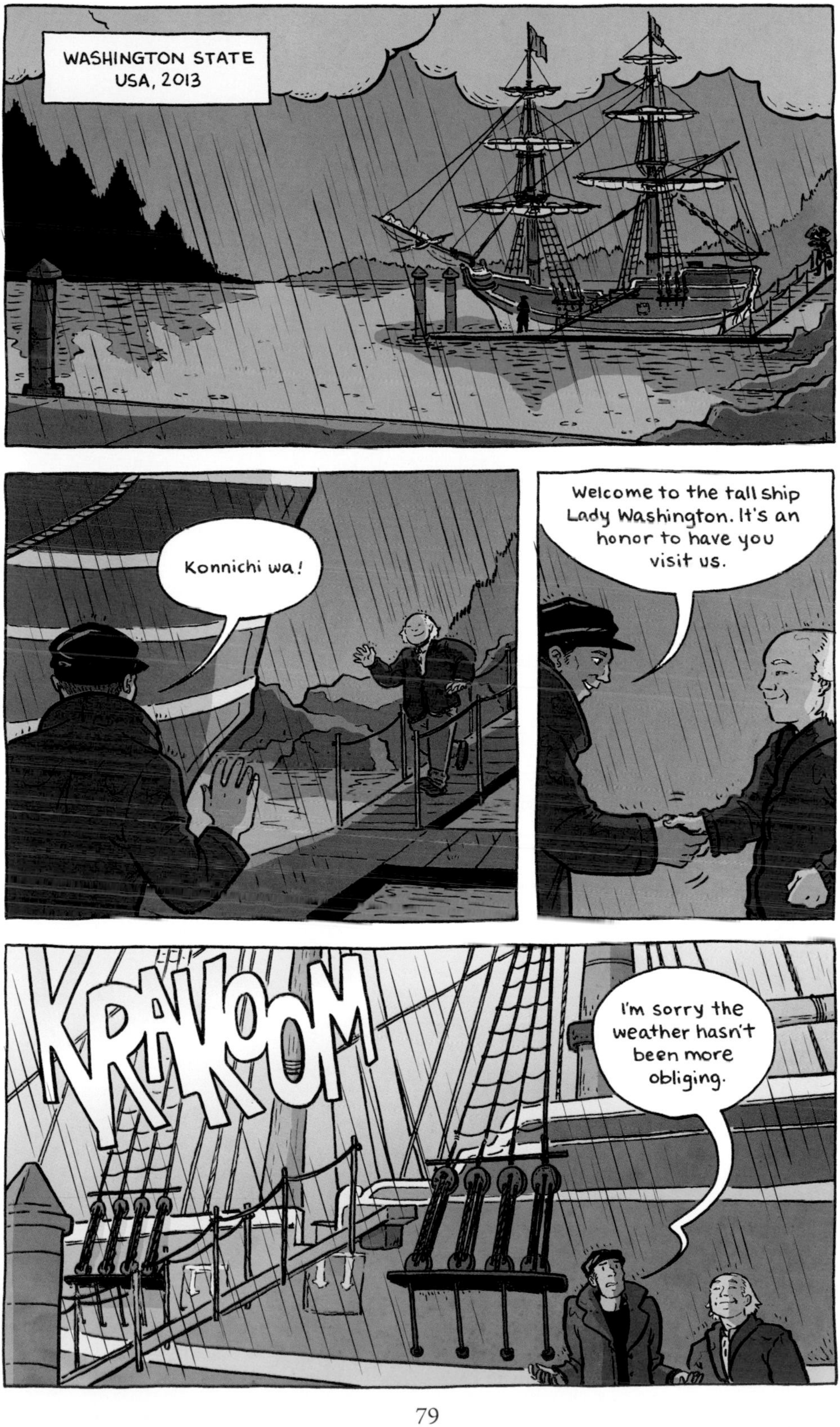
WASHINGTON STATE
USA, 2013
Konnichi wa!
Welcome to the tall ship Lady Washington. It's an honor to have you visit us.
KRAKOOM
I'm sorry the weather hasn't been more obliging.

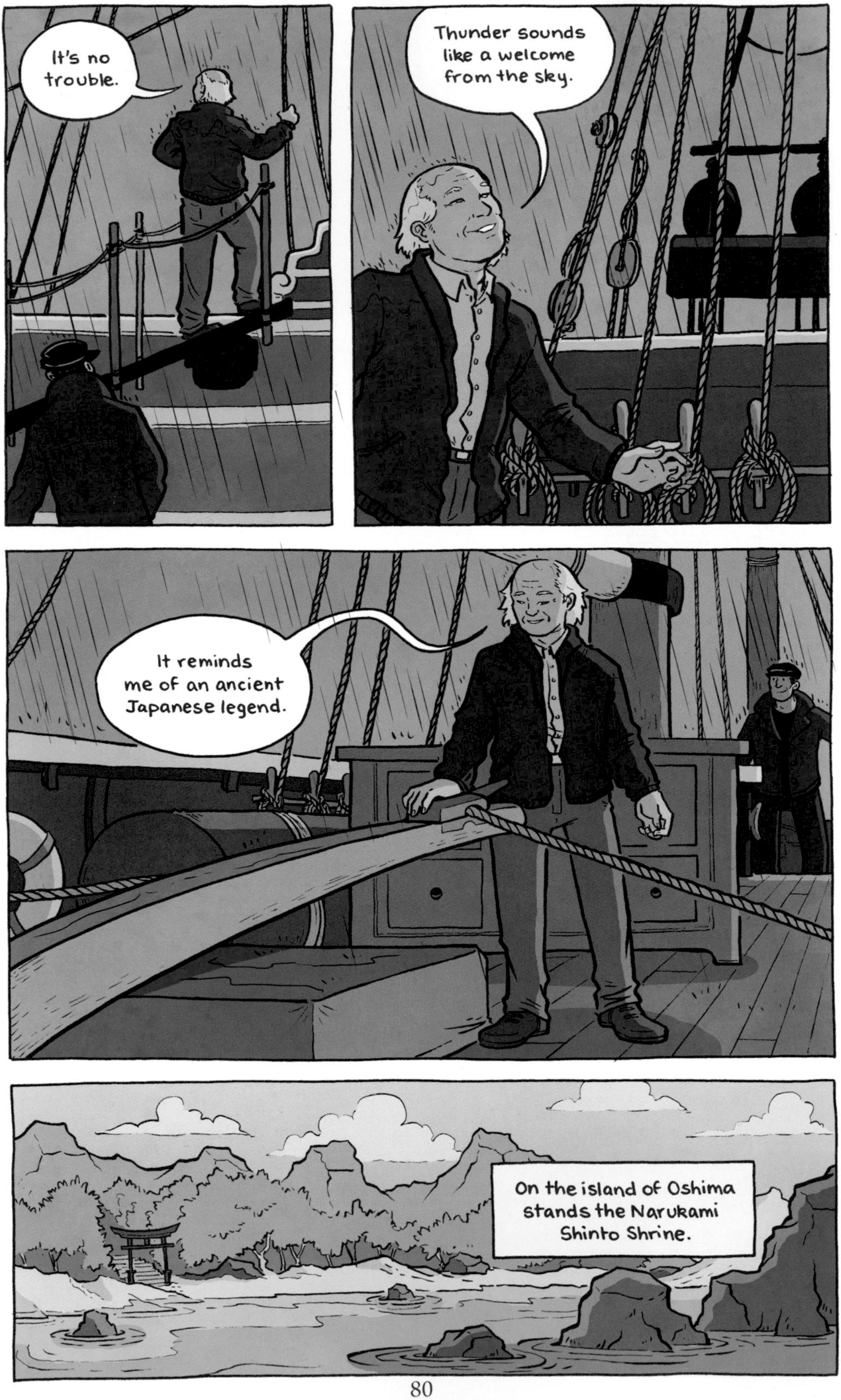
It's no trouble.
Thunder sounds like a welcome from the sky.
It reminds me of an ancient Japanese legend.
On the island of Oshima stands the Narukami Shinto Shrine.

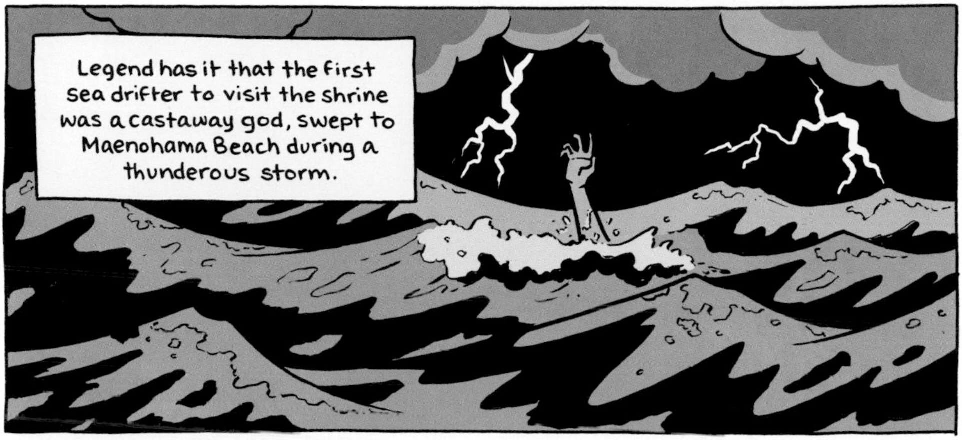
Legend has it that the first sea drifter to visit the shrine was a castaway god, swept to Maenohama Beach during a thunderous storm.

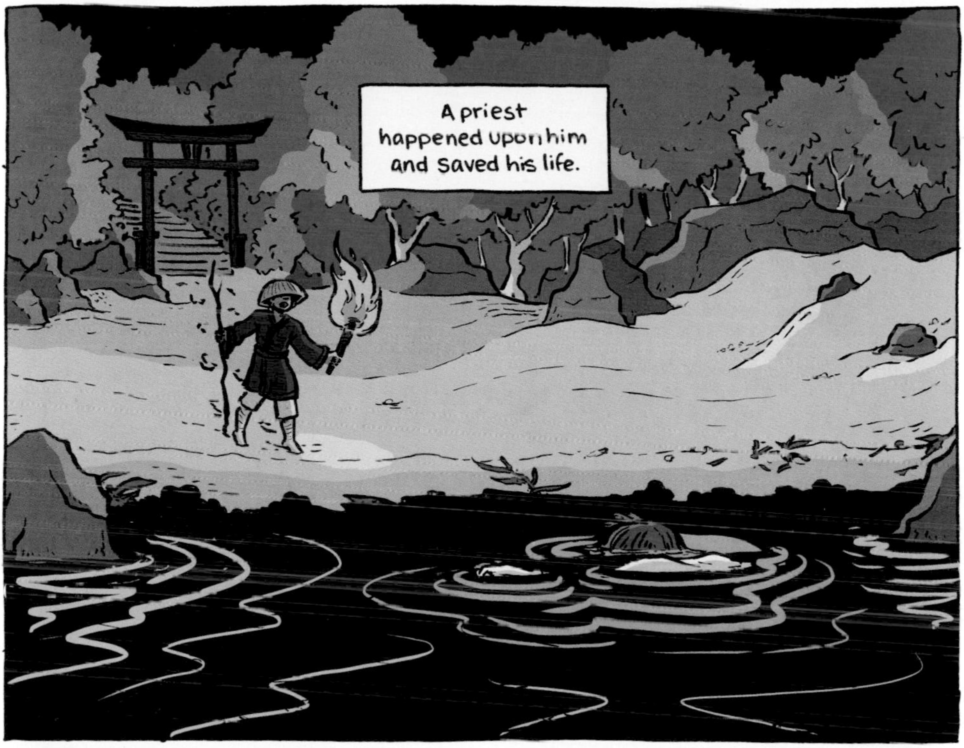
A priest happened upon him and saved his life.

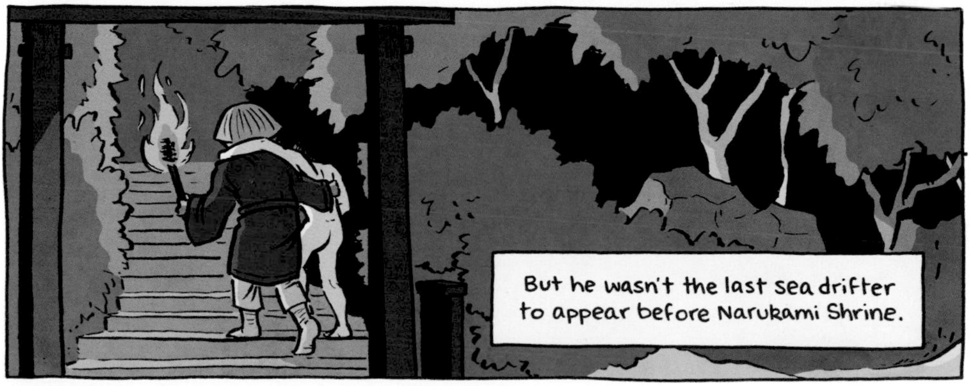
But he wasn't the last sea drifter to appear before Narukami Shrine.

Centuries passed, and one spring day in 1791, two foreign vessels arrived in the Kumano-nada Sea flying unfamiliar flags.

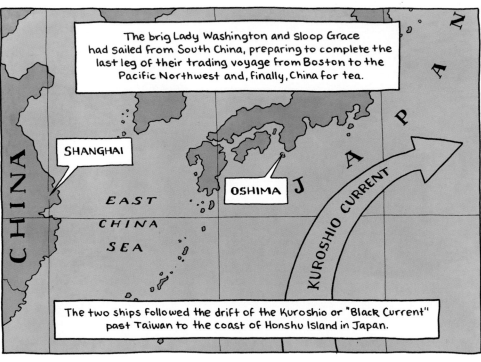

The brig Lady Washington and sloop Grace had sailed from South China, preparing to complete the last leg of their trading voyage from Boston to the Pacific Northwest and, finally, China for tea.

CHINA

JAPAN

SHANGHAI

OSHIMA

EAST CHINA SEA

KUROSHIO CURRENT

The two ships followed the drift of the Kuroshio or "Black Current" past Taiwan to the coast of Honshu Island in Japan.

All trade with foreigners was forbidden at the time, but Captain Kendrick's employers had other ideas.

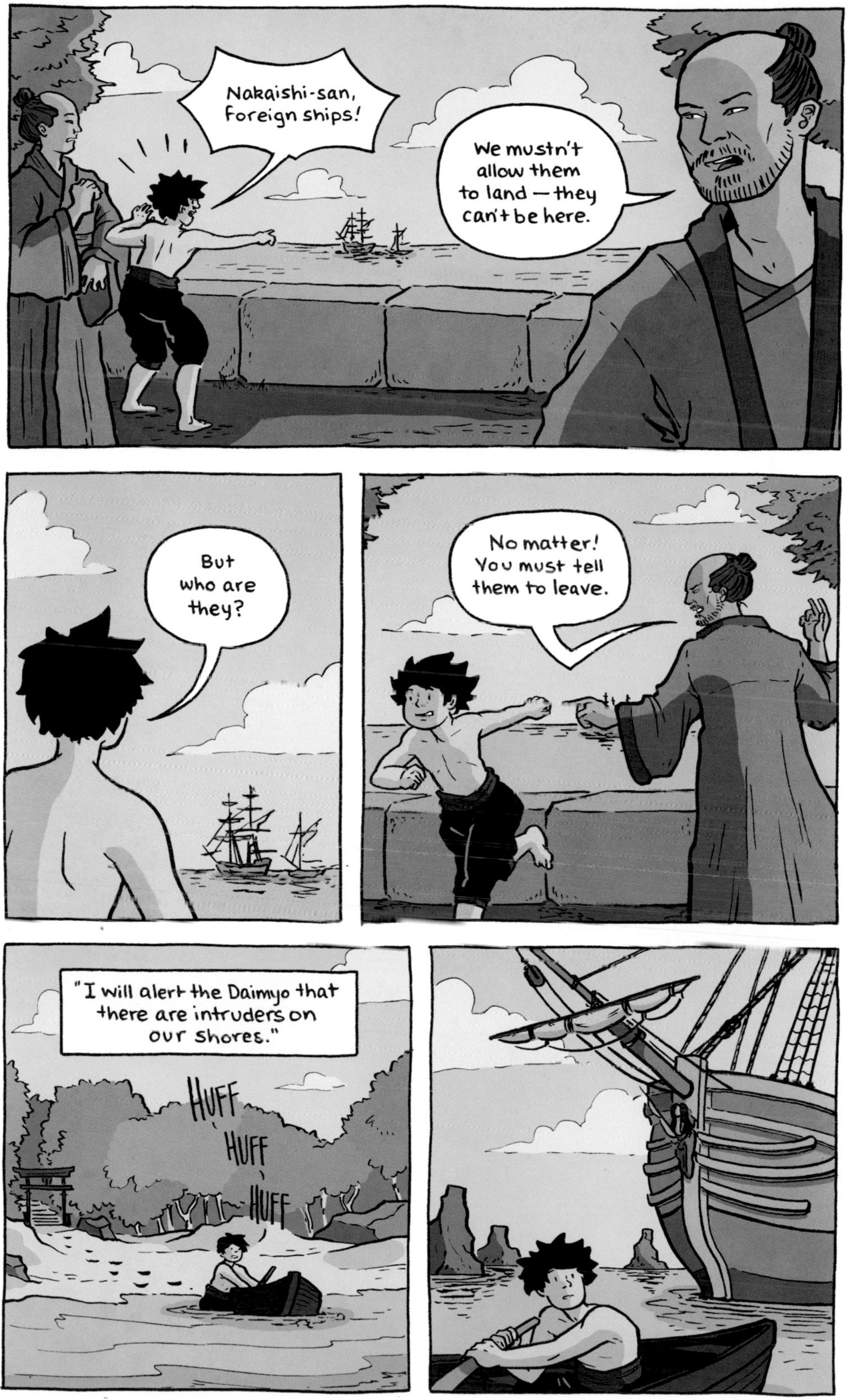
Nakaishi-san, foreign ships!
We mustn't allow them to land — they can't be here.
But who are they?
No matter! You must tell them to leave.
"I will alert the Daimyo that there are intruders on our shores."
HUFF
HUFF
HUFF

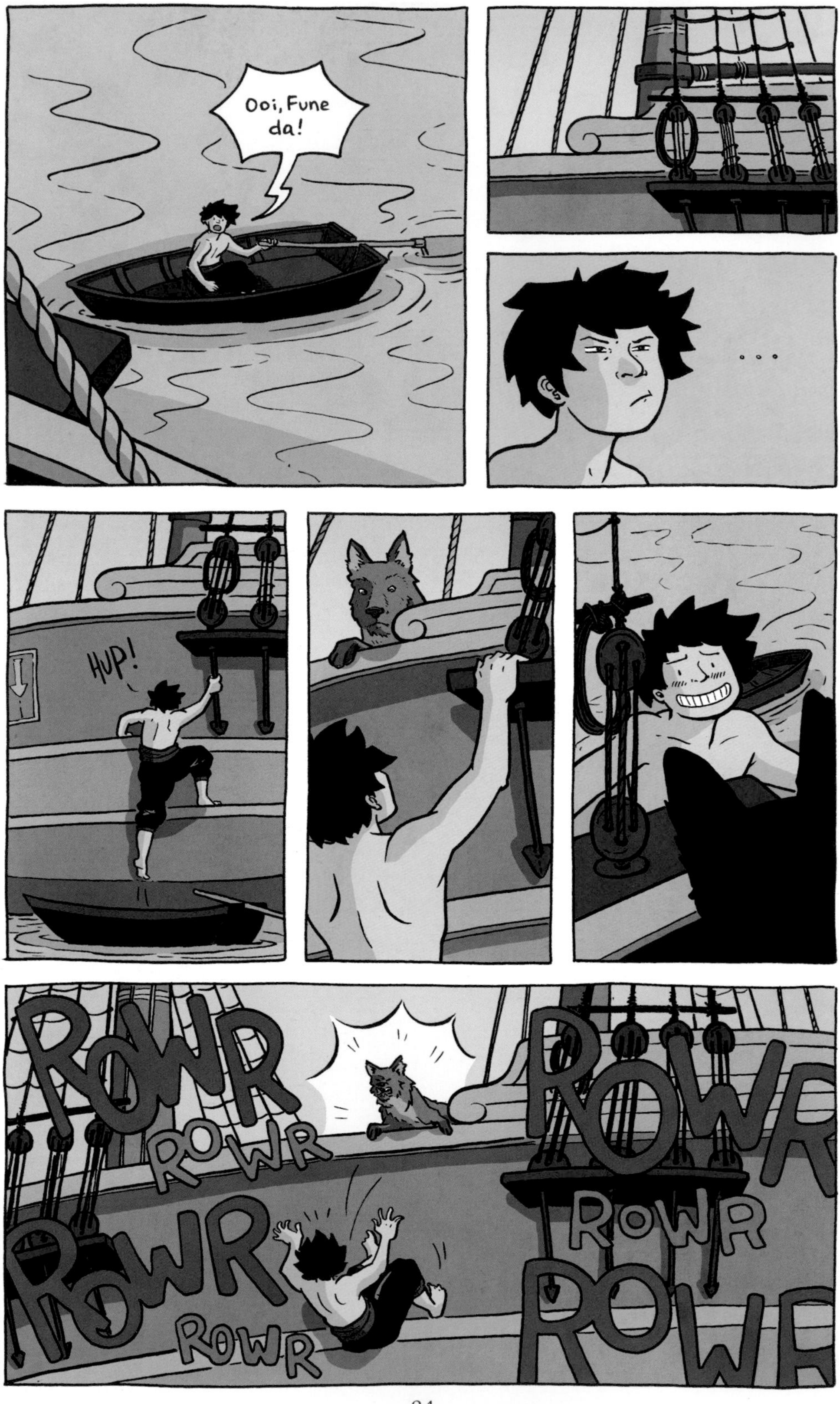
Ooi, Fune da!
...
HUP!
ROWR
ROWR
ROWR
ROWR
ROWR
ROWR
ROWR
ROWR

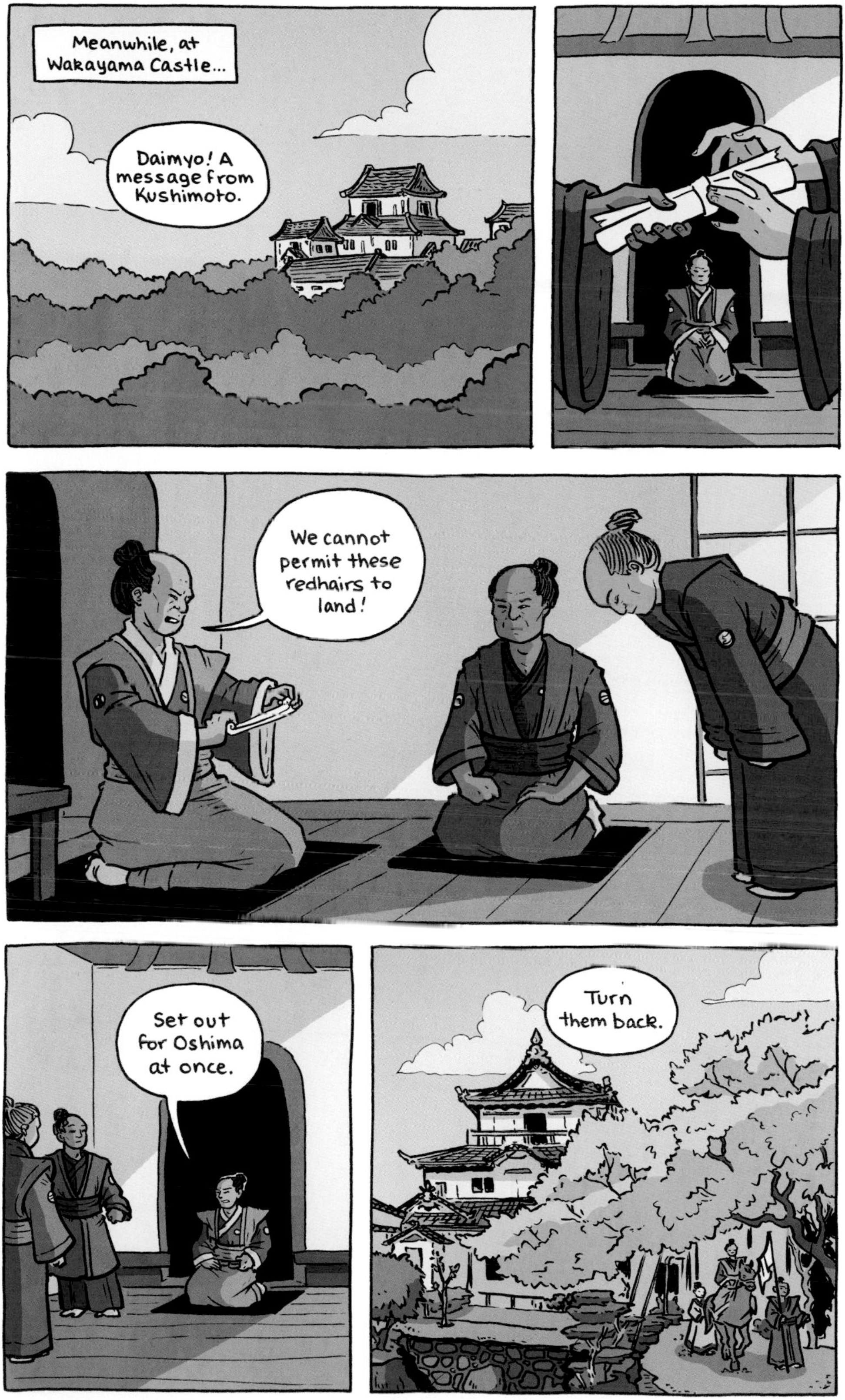
Meanwhile, at Wakayama Castle...
Daimyo! A message from Kushimoto.
We cannot permit these redhairs to land!
Set out for Oshima at once.
Turn them back.

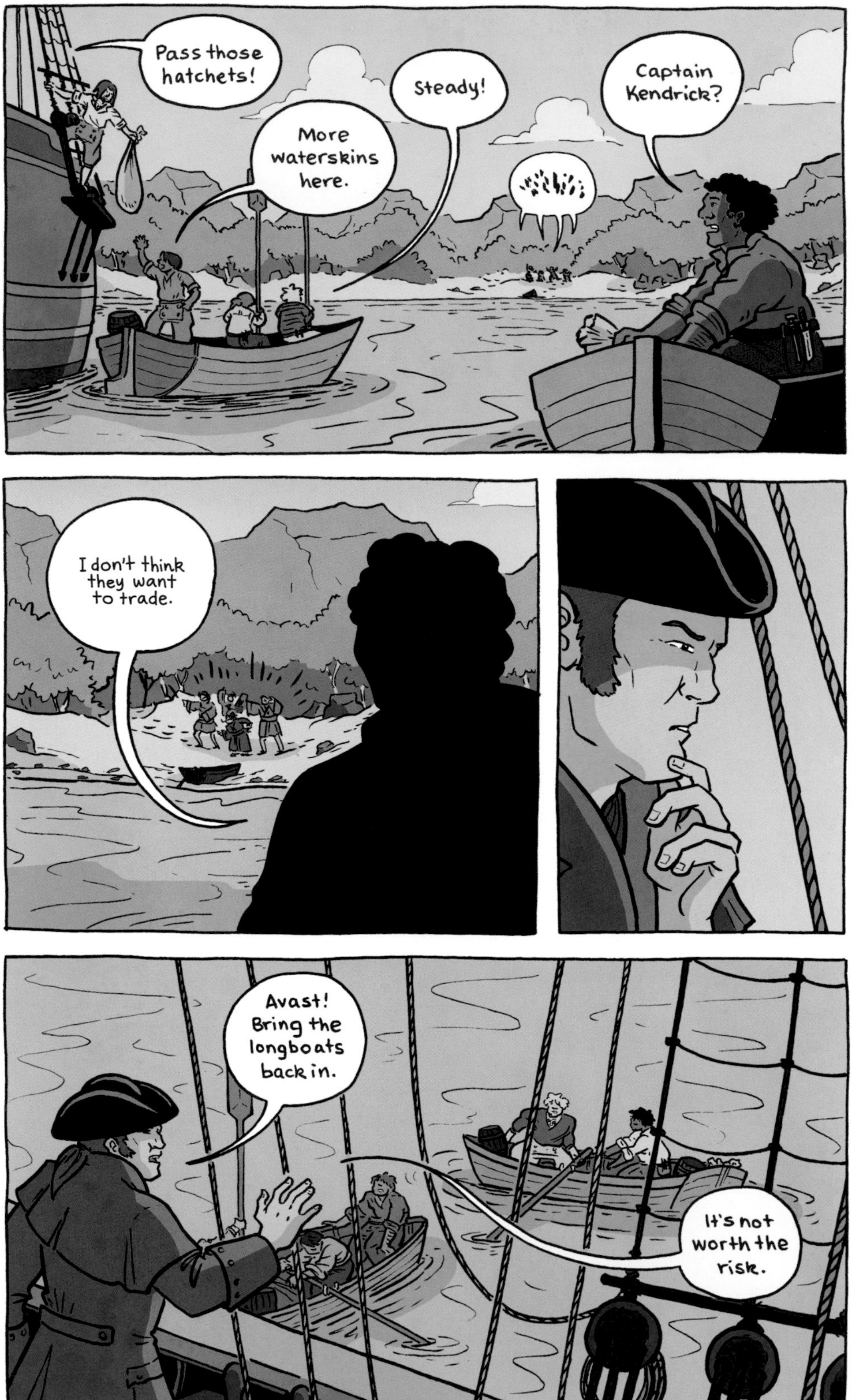
Pass those hatchets!
More waterskins here.
Steady!
Captain Kendrick?
I don't think they want to trade.
Avast! Bring the longboats back in.
It's not worth the risk.

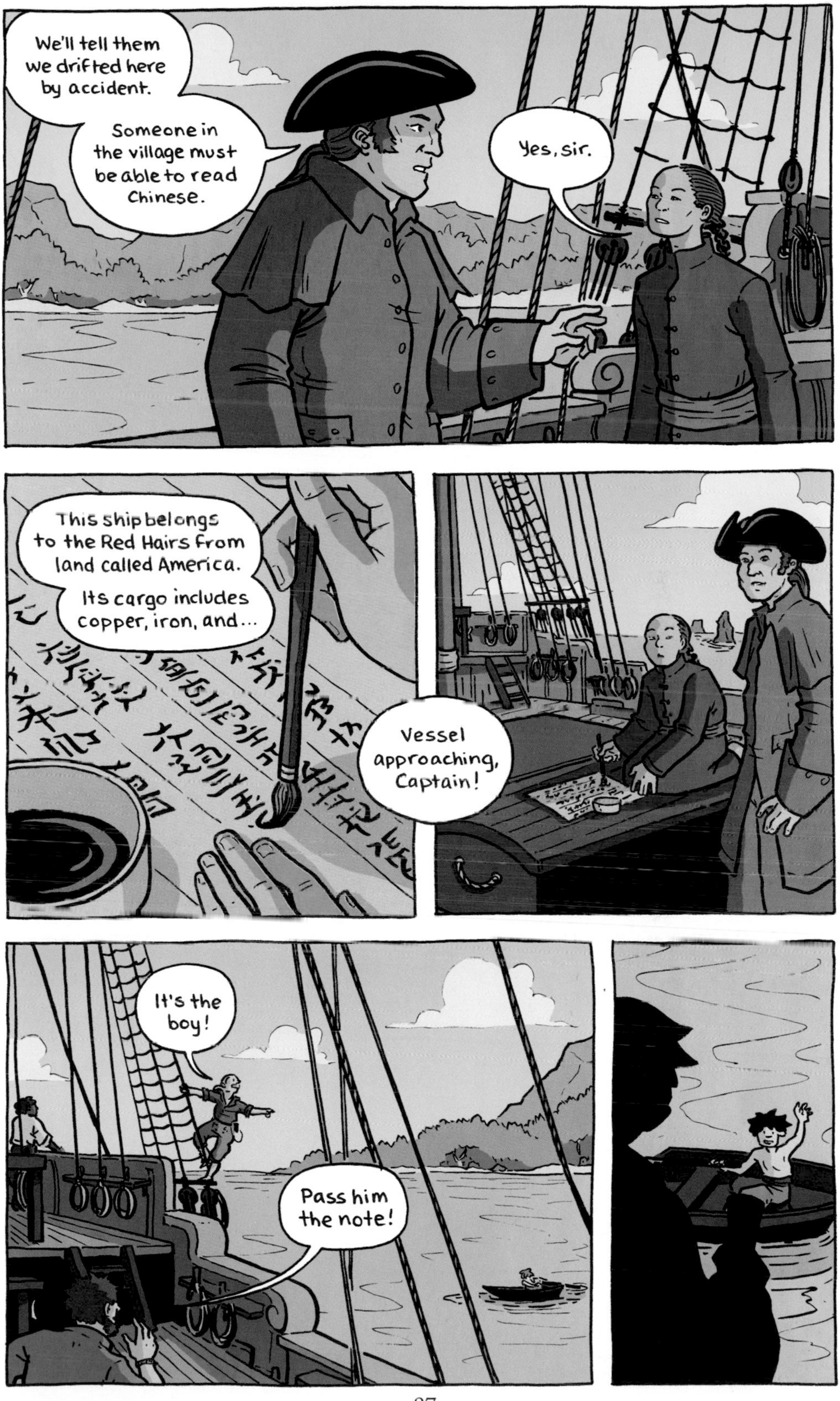
We'll tell them we drifted here by accident.
Someone in the village must be able to read Chinese.
Yes, sir.
This ship belongs to the Red Hairs from land called America.
Its cargo includes copper, iron, and...
Vessel approaching, Captain!
It's the boy!
Pass him the note!

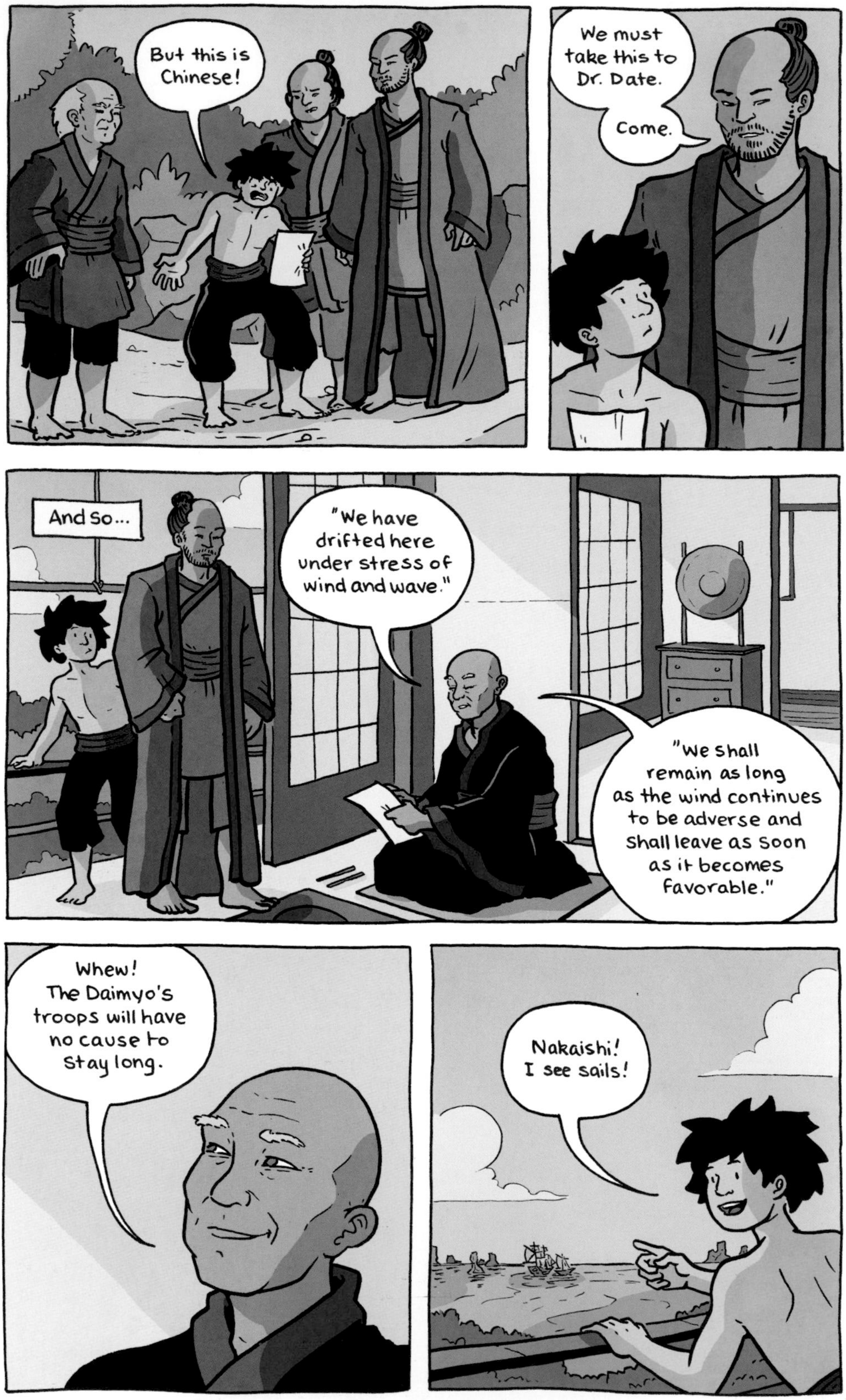
But this is Chinese!
We must take this to Dr. Date.
Come.
And so...
"We have drifted here under stress of wind and wave."
"We shall remain as long as the wind continues to be adverse and shall leave as soon as it becomes favorable."
Whew! The Daimyo's troops will have no cause to stay long.
Nakaishi! I see sails!

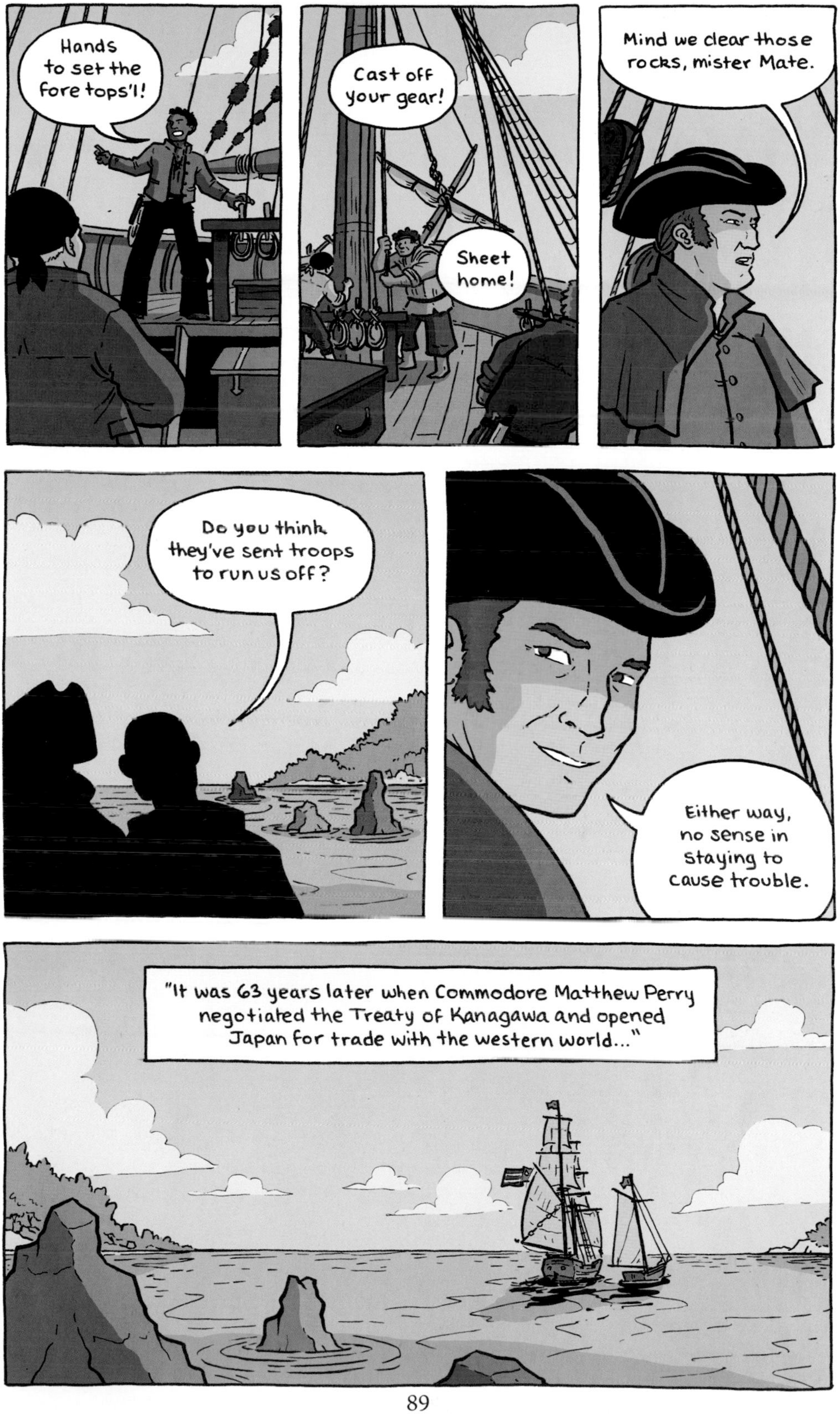
Hands to set the fore tops'l!
Cast off your gear!
Sheet home!
Mind we clear those rocks, mister Mate.
Do you think they've sent troops to run us off?
Either way, no sense in staying to cause trouble.
"It was 63 years later when Commodore Matthew Perry negotiated the Treaty of Kanagawa and opened Japan for trade with the western world..."

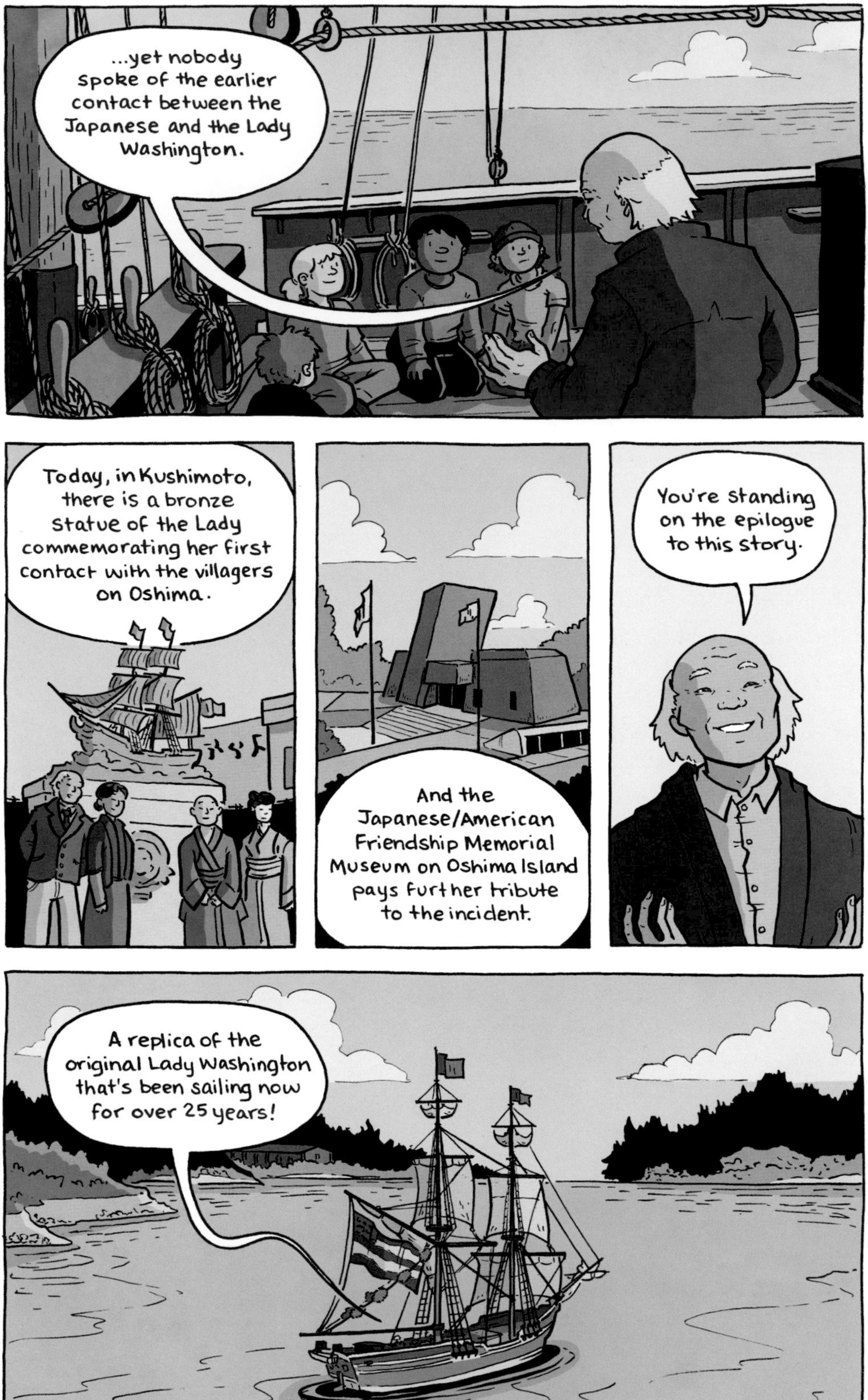
...yet nobody spoke of the earlier contact between the Japanese and the Lady Washington.
Today, in Kushimoto, there is a bronze statue of the Lady commemorating her first contact with the villagers on Oshima.
And the Japanese/American Friendship Memorial Museum on Oshima Island pays further tribute to the incident.
You're standing on the epilogue to this story.
A replica of the original Lady Washington that's been sailing now for over 25 years!

GLOSSARY

USE THIS JAPANESE-ENGLISH GLOSSARY TO EXPAND YOUR VOCABULARY!

kaminari = thunder
zaa zaa = sound of heavy rain
goro goro = rumbling of thunder
Kuroshio = Black Current
(North Pacific Current)
ureshii = happy
ikokusen = foreign ship
Kurofune = black ship (steam frigate)
Torii = Shinto Shrine gate
owari = the end
Sayonara = goodbye!

Scurvy

Dogs

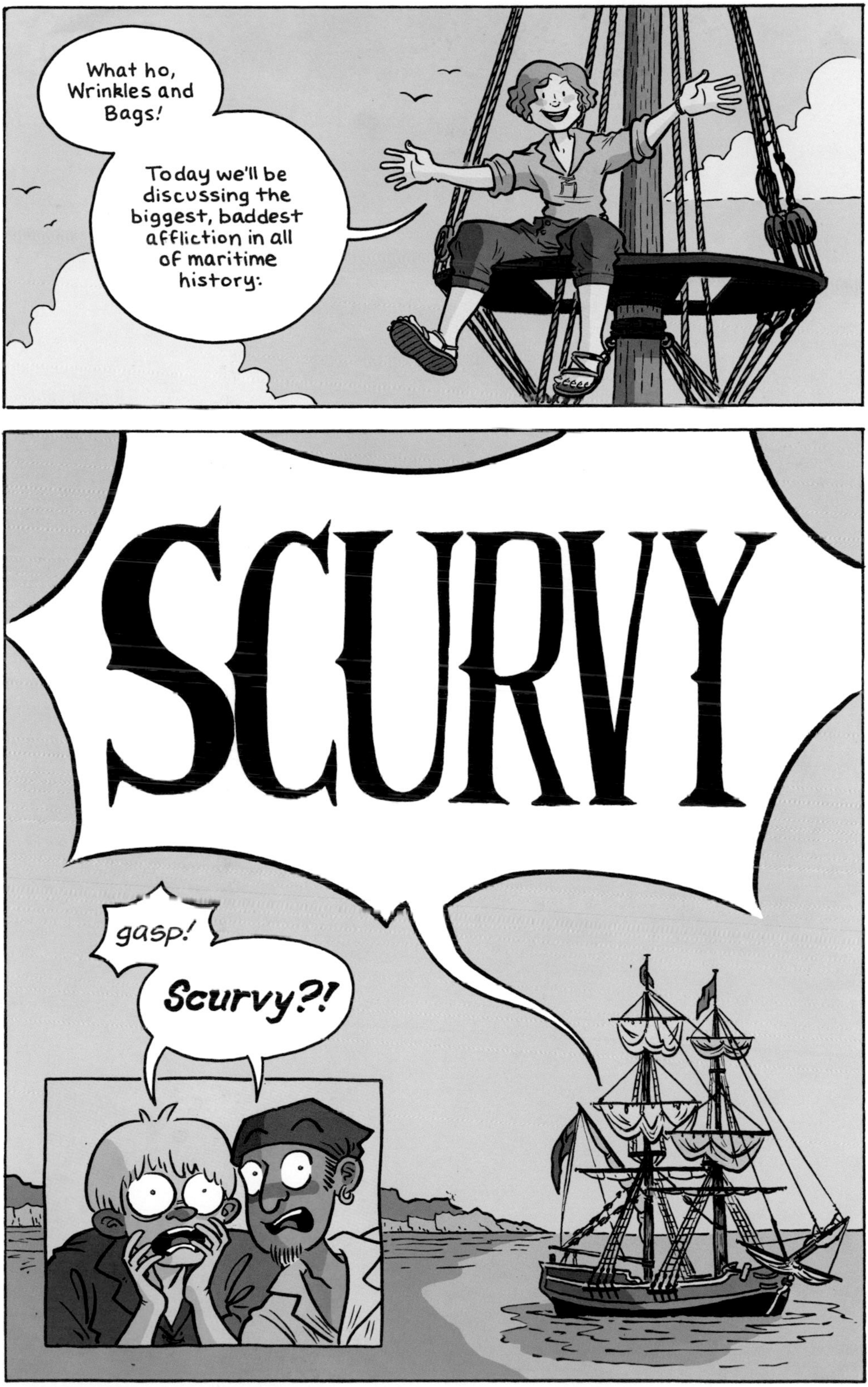
What ho, Wrinkles and Bags!
Today we'll be discussing the biggest, baddest affliction in all of maritime history:
SCURVY
gasp!
Scurvy?!

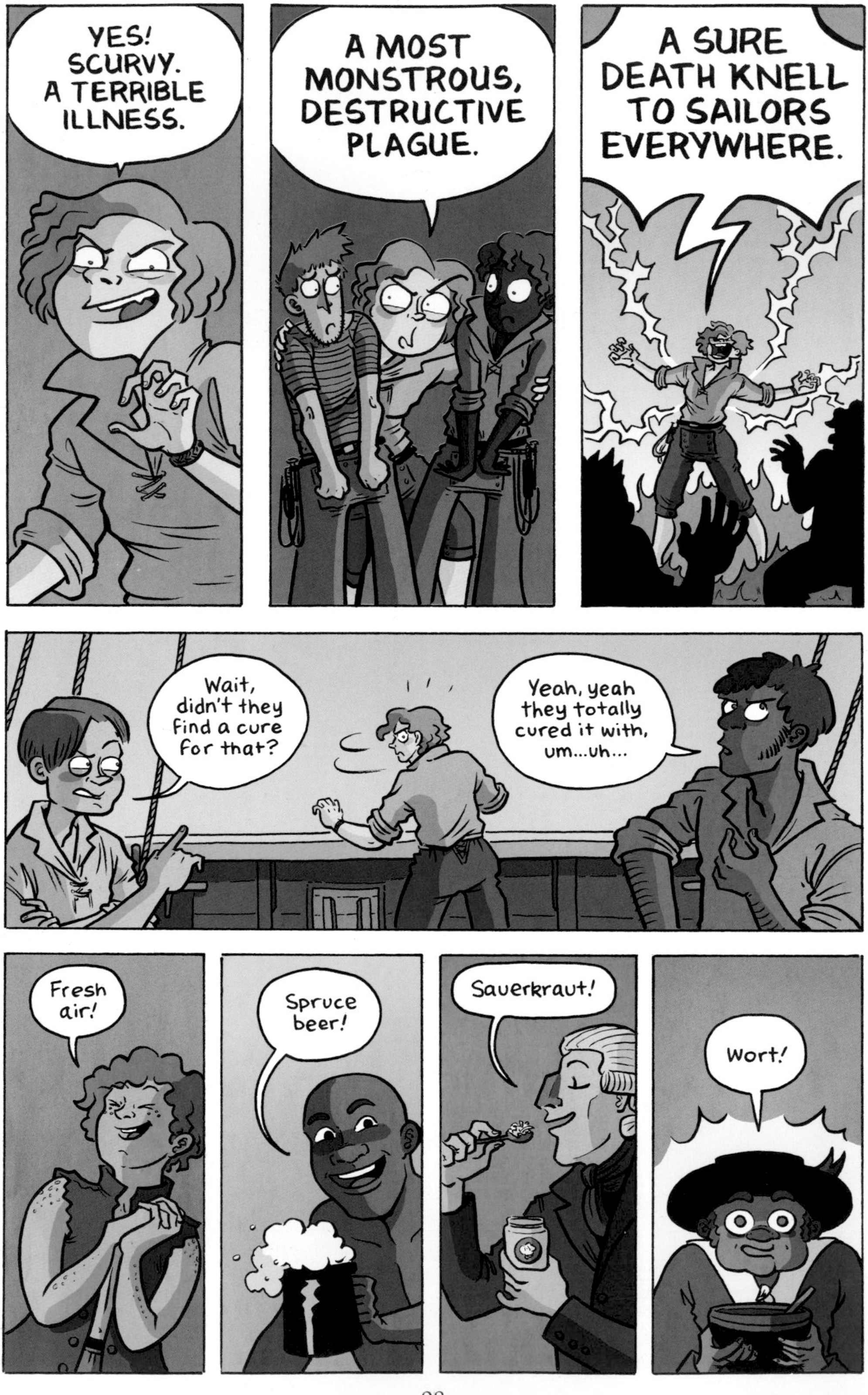
YES! SCURVY. A TERRIBLE ILLNESS.
A MOST MONSTROUS, DESTRUCTIVE PLAGUE.
A SURE DEATH KNELL TO SAILORS EVERYWHERE.
Wait, didn't they find a cure for that?
Yeah, yeah they totally cured it with, um...uh...
Fresh air!
Spruce beer!
Sauerkraut!
Wort!

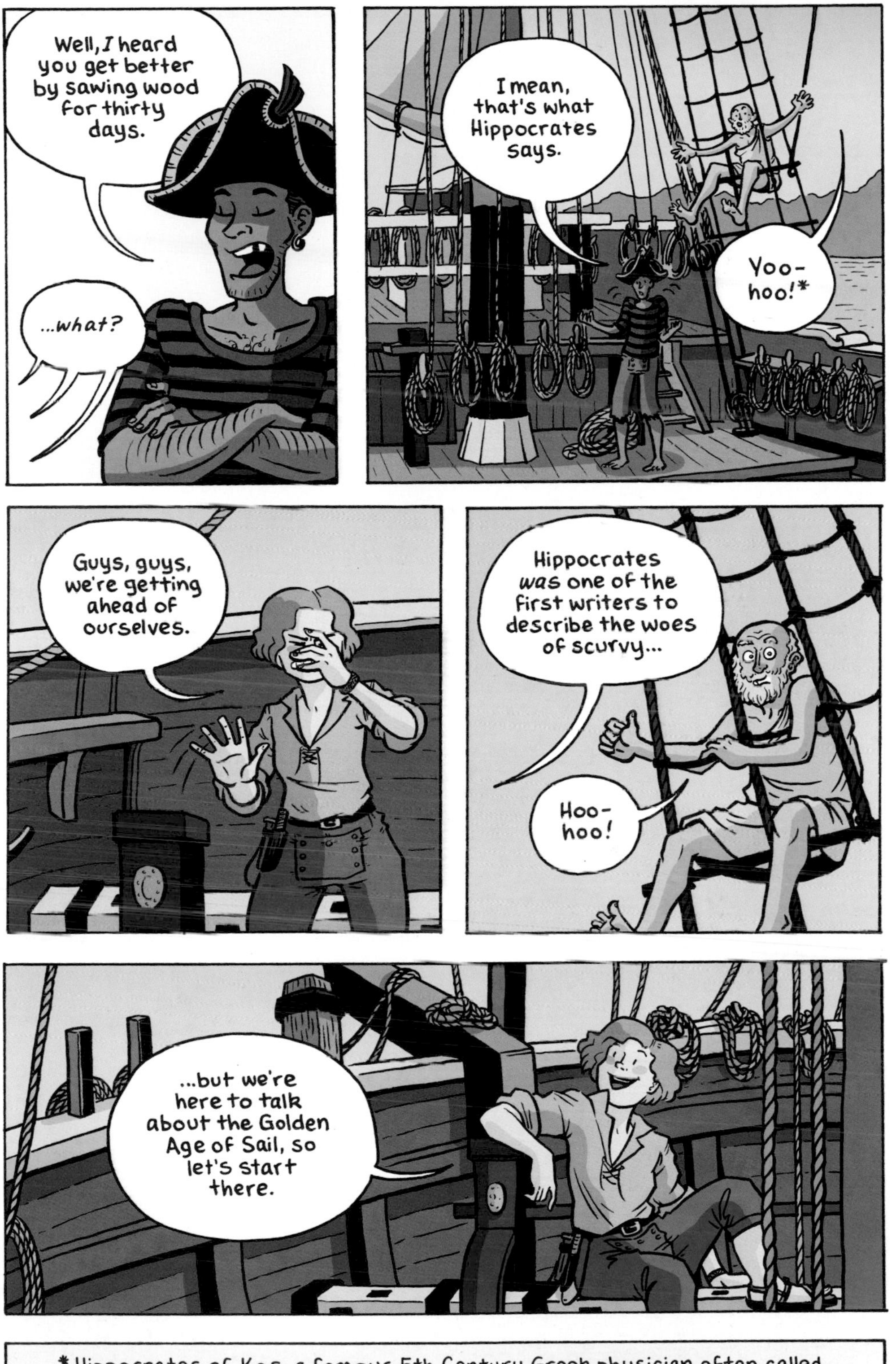
Well, *I* heard you get better by sawing wood for thirty days.
...what?
I mean, that's what Hippocrates says.
Yoo-hoo!*
Guys, guys, we're getting ahead of ourselves.
Hippocrates *was* one of the first writers to describe the woes of scurvy...
Hoo-hoo!
...but we're here to talk about the Golden Age of Sail, so let's start there.

* Hippocrates of Kos, a famous 5th Century Greek physician often called the "Father of Western Medicine," had some weird ideas about scurvy.

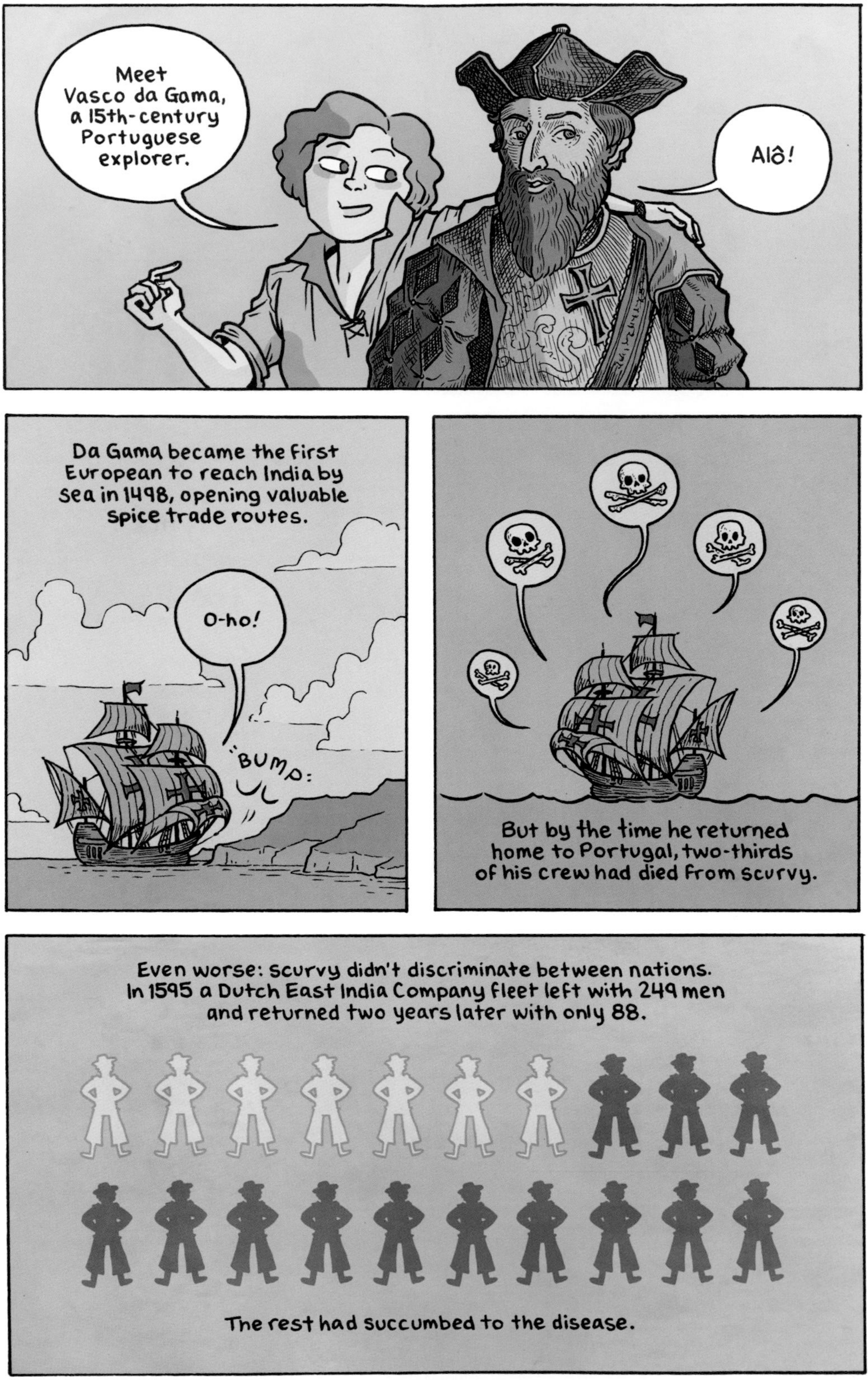
Meet Vasco da Gama, a 15th-century Portuguese explorer.
Alô!
Da Gama became the first European to reach India by sea in 1498, opening valuable spice trade routes.
O-ho!
BUMP
But by the time he returned home to Portugal, two-thirds of his crew had died from scurvy.
Even worse: scurvy didn't discriminate between nations. In 1595 a Dutch East India Company fleet left with 249 men and returned two years later with only 88.
The rest had succumbed to the disease.

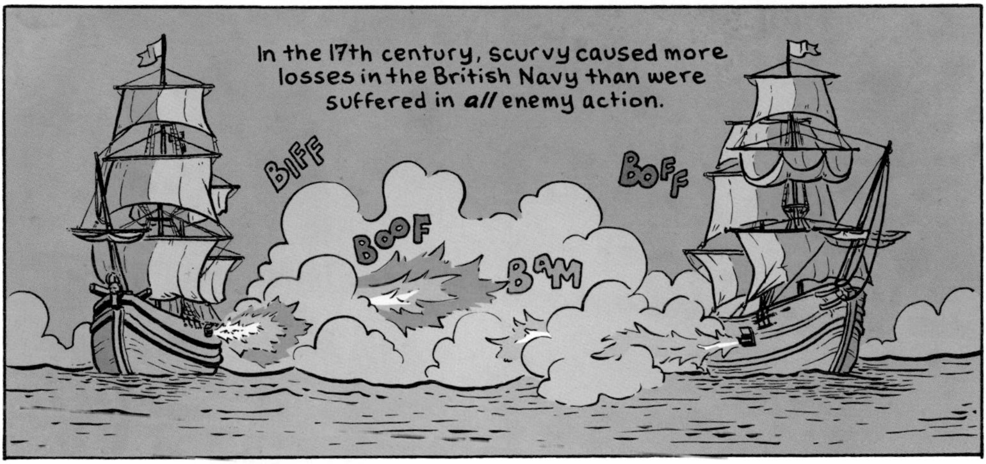
In the 17th century, scurvy caused more losses in the British Navy than were suffered in *all* enemy action.
BIFF
BOOF
BAM
BOFF

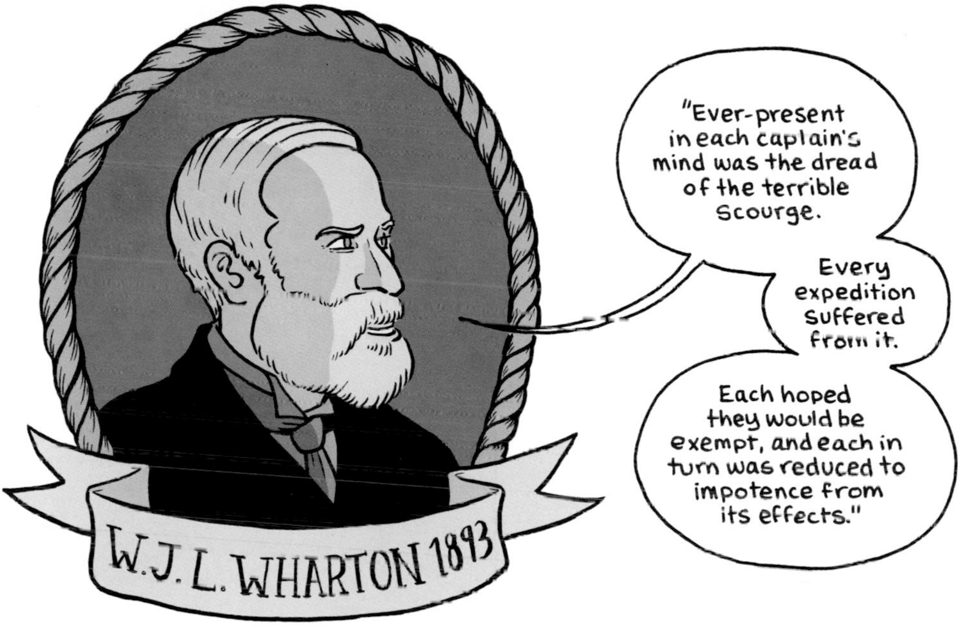
"Ever-present in each captain's mind was the dread of the terrible scourge.
Every expedition suffered from it.
Each hoped they would be exempt, and each in turn was reduced to impotence from its effects."
W.J.L. WHARTON 1893

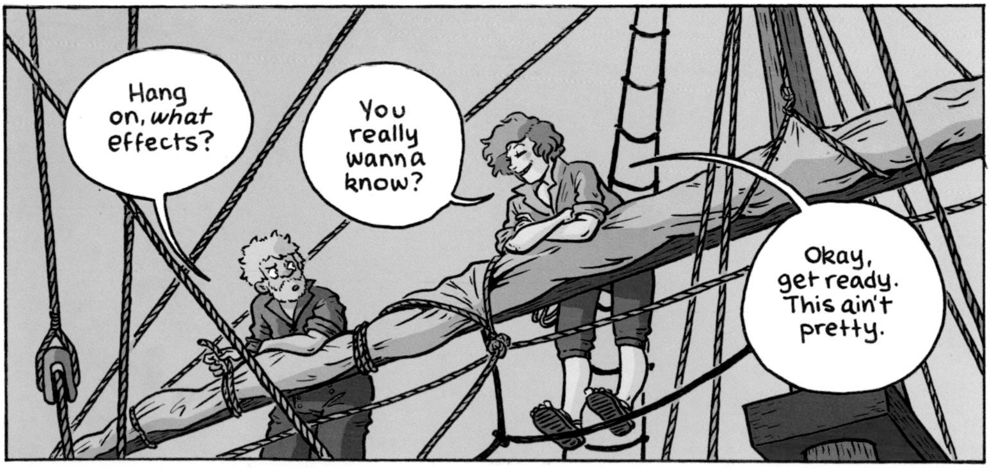
Hang on, *what* effects?
You really wanna know?
Okay, get ready. This ain't pretty.

HOW TO SCURVY

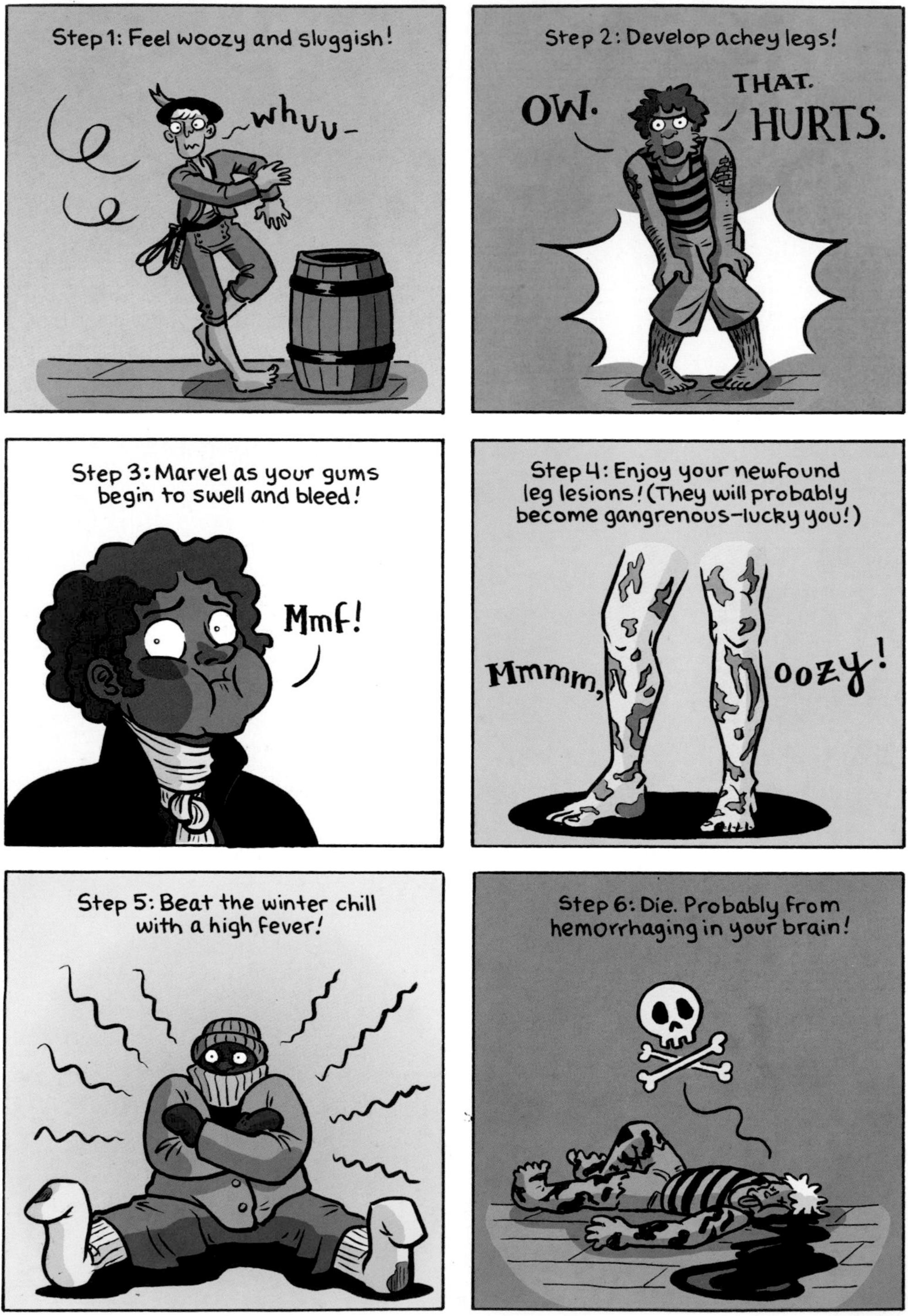
Step 1: Feel woozy and sluggish!
whuu-
Step 2: Develop achey legs!
OW.
THAT. HURTS.
Step 3: Marvel as your gums begin to swell and bleed!
Mmf!
Step 4: Enjoy your newfound leg lesions! (They will probably become gangrenous-lucky you!)
Mmmm, oozy!
Step 5: Beat the winter chill with a high fever!
Step 6: Die. Probably from hemorrhaging in your brain!

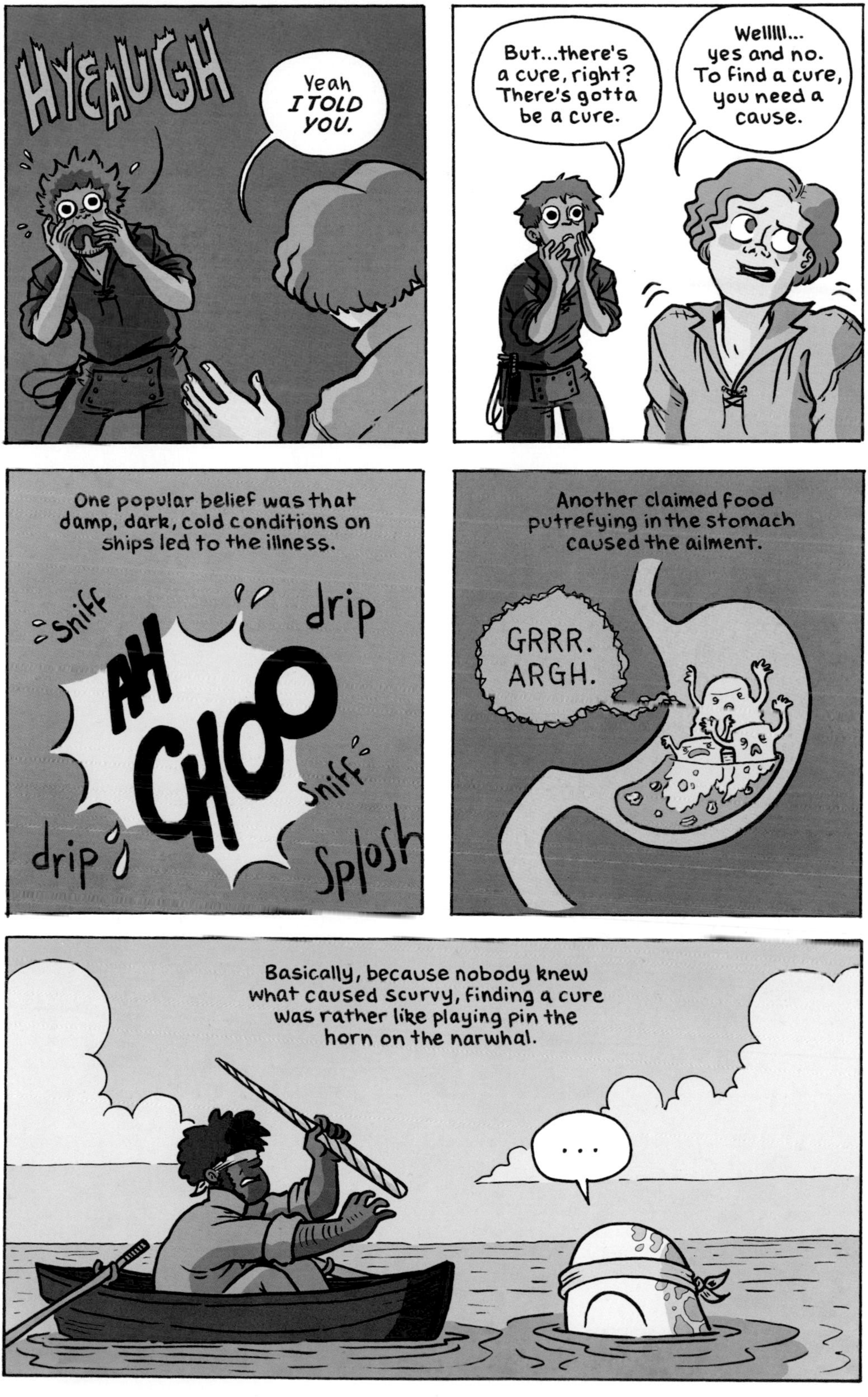
HYEAUGH
Yeah I TOLD YOU.
But...there's a cure, right? There's gotta be a cure.
Welllll... yes and no. To find a cure, you need a cause.
One popular belief was that damp, dark, cold conditions on ships led to the illness.
Sniff
drip
AH CHOO
Sniff
drip
Splosh
Another claimed food putrefying in the stomach caused the ailment.
GRRR. ARGH.
Basically, because nobody knew what caused scurvy, finding a cure was rather like playing pin the horn on the narwhal.
...

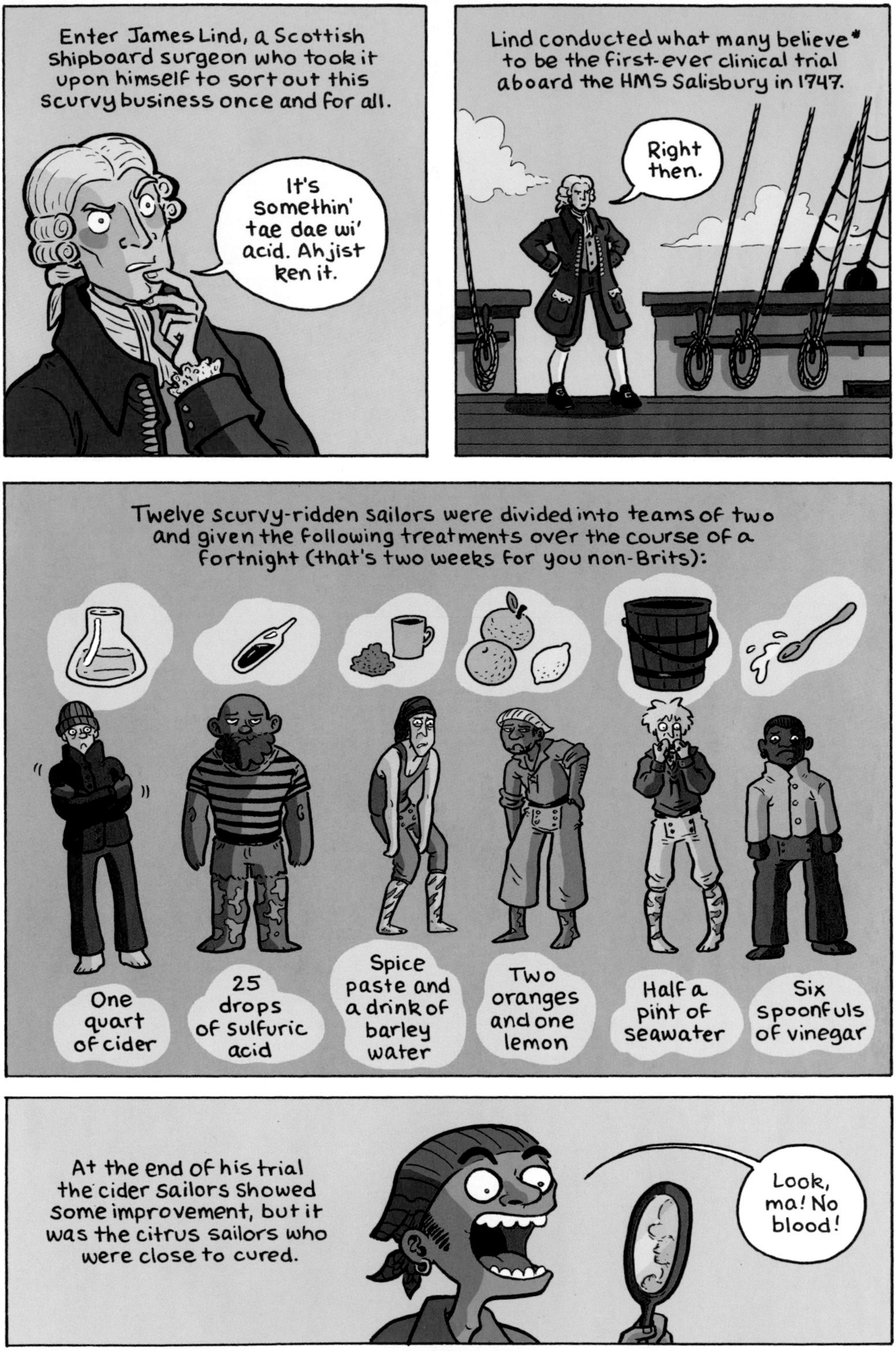
Enter James Lind, a Scottish shipboard surgeon who took it upon himself to sort out this scurvy business once and for all.
It's somethin' tae dae wi' acid. Ahjist ken it.
Lind conducted what many believe* to be the first-ever clinical trial aboard the HMS Salisbury in 1747.
Right then.
Twelve scurvy-ridden sailors were divided into teams of two and given the following treatments over the course of a fortnight (that's two weeks for you non-Brits):
One quart of cider
25 drops of sulfuric acid
Spice paste and a drink of barley water
Two oranges and one lemon
Half a pint of seawater
Six spoonfuls of vinegar
At the end of his trial the cider sailors showed some improvement, but it was the citrus sailors who were close to cured.
Look, ma! No blood!

*Jeremy Hugh-Baron, a modern Oxford historian, disputes this claim.

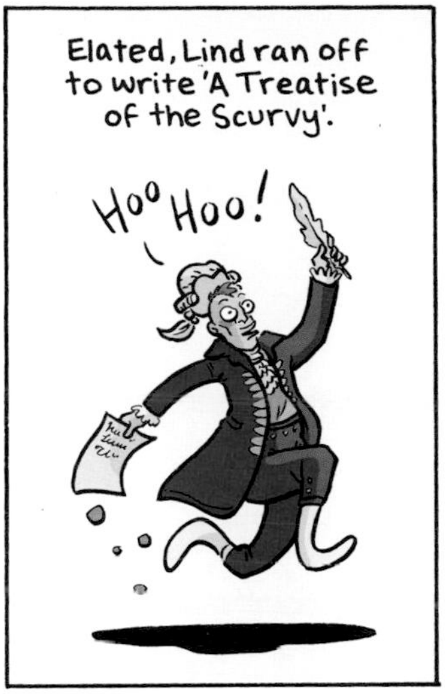
Elated, Lind ran off to write 'A Treatise of the Scurvy'.
Hoo Hoo!

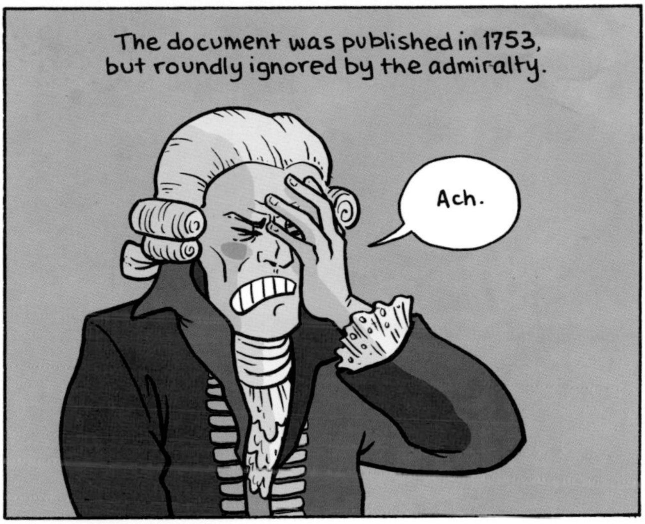
The document was published in 1753, but roundly ignored by the admiralty.
Ach.

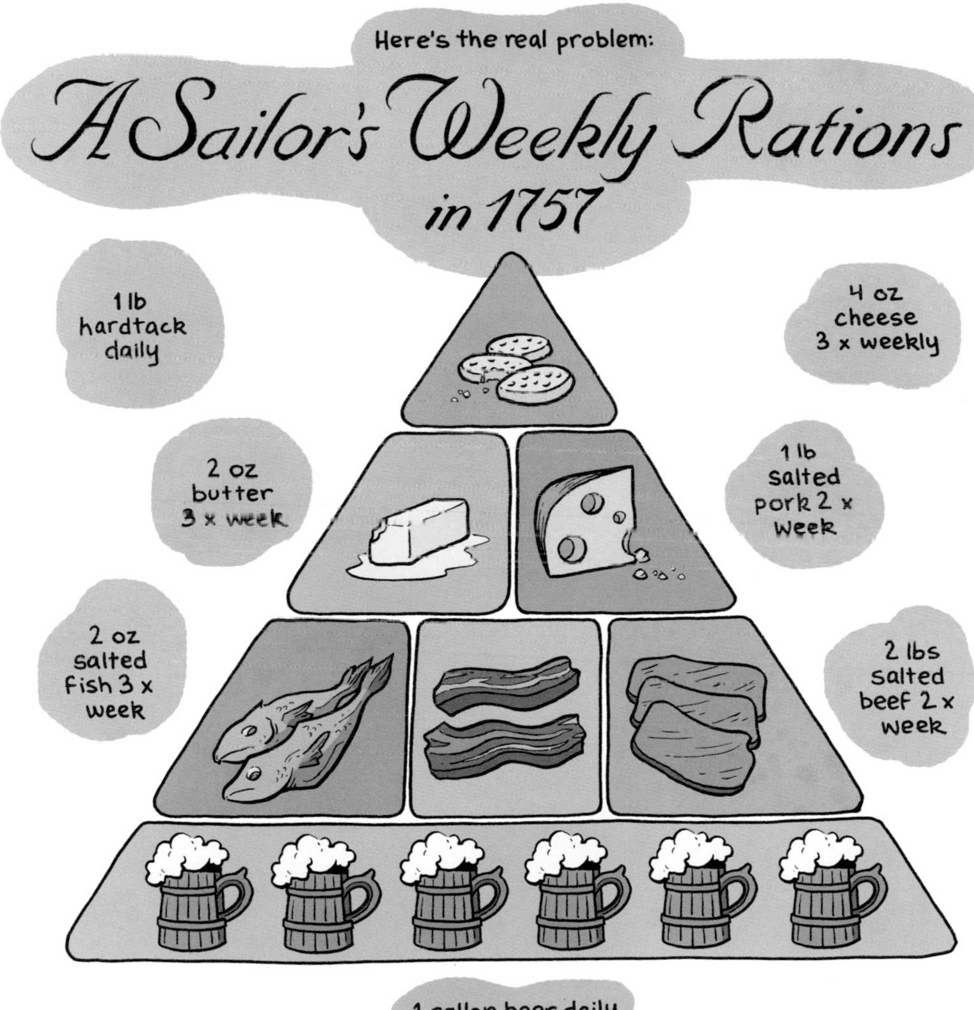
Here's the real problem:
A Sailor's Weekly Rations in 1757
1 lb hardtack daily
4 oz cheese 3 x weekly
2 oz butter 3 x week
1 lb salted pork 2 x week
2 oz salted fish 3 x week
2 lbs salted beef 2 x week
1 gallon beer daily

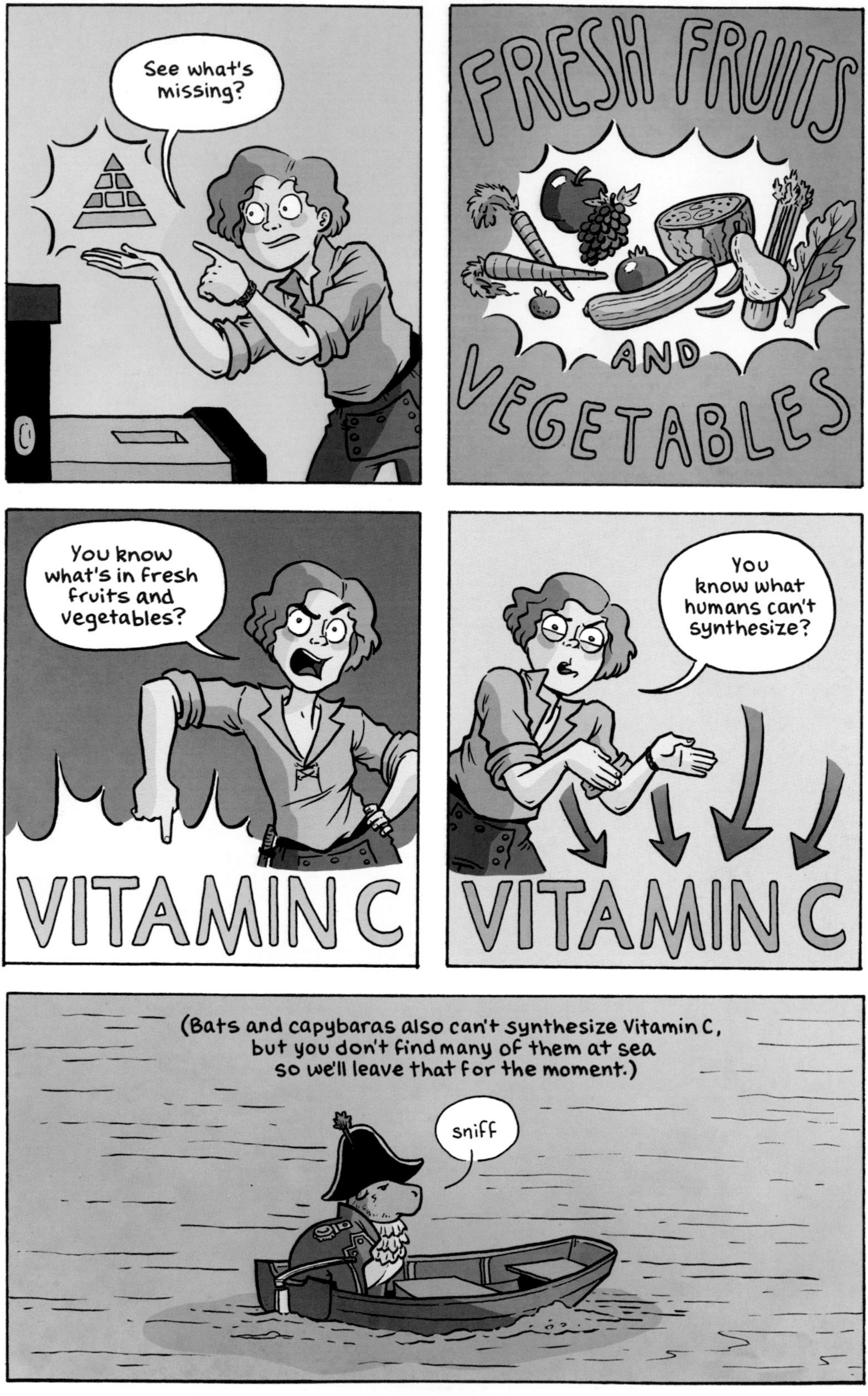
See what's missing?
FRESH FRUITS
AND
VEGETABLES
You know what's in fresh fruits and vegetables?
VITAMIN C
You know what humans can't synthesize?
VITAMIN C
(Bats and capybaras also can't synthesize Vitamin C, but you don't find many of them at sea so we'll leave that for the moment.)
sniff

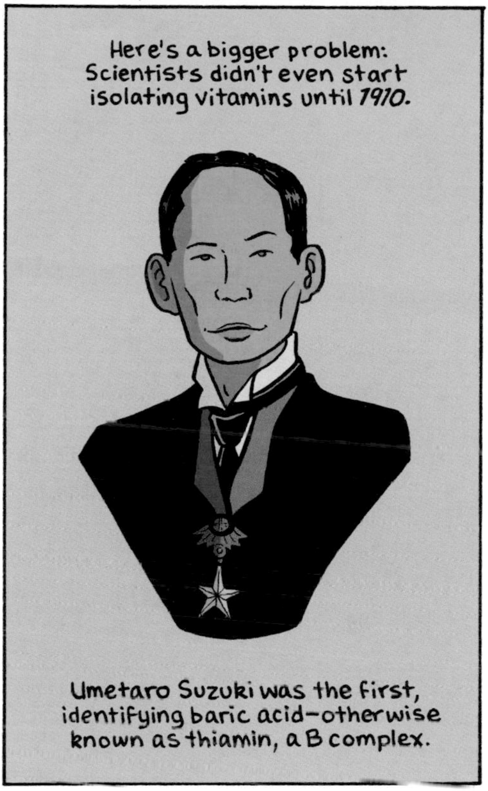
Here's a bigger problem: Scientists didn't even start isolating vitamins until 1910.
Umetaro Suzuki was the first, identifying baric acid—otherwise known as thiamin, a B complex.

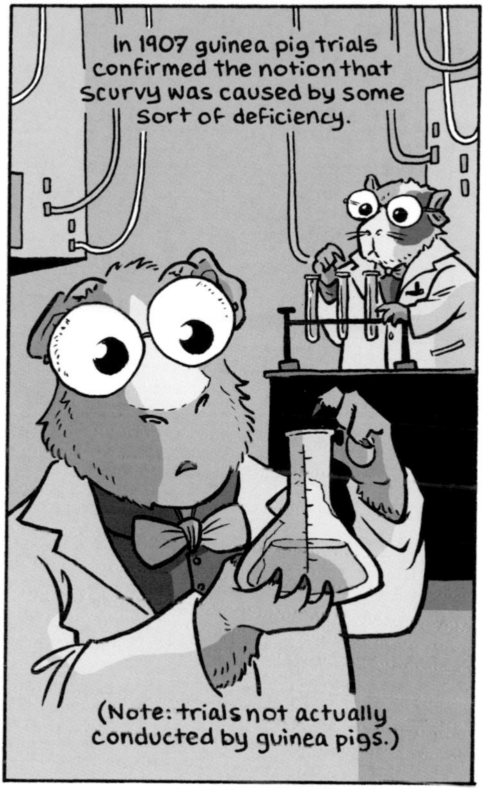
In 1907 guinea pig trials confirmed the notion that scurvy was caused by some sort of deficiency.
(Note: trials not actually conducted by guinea pigs.)

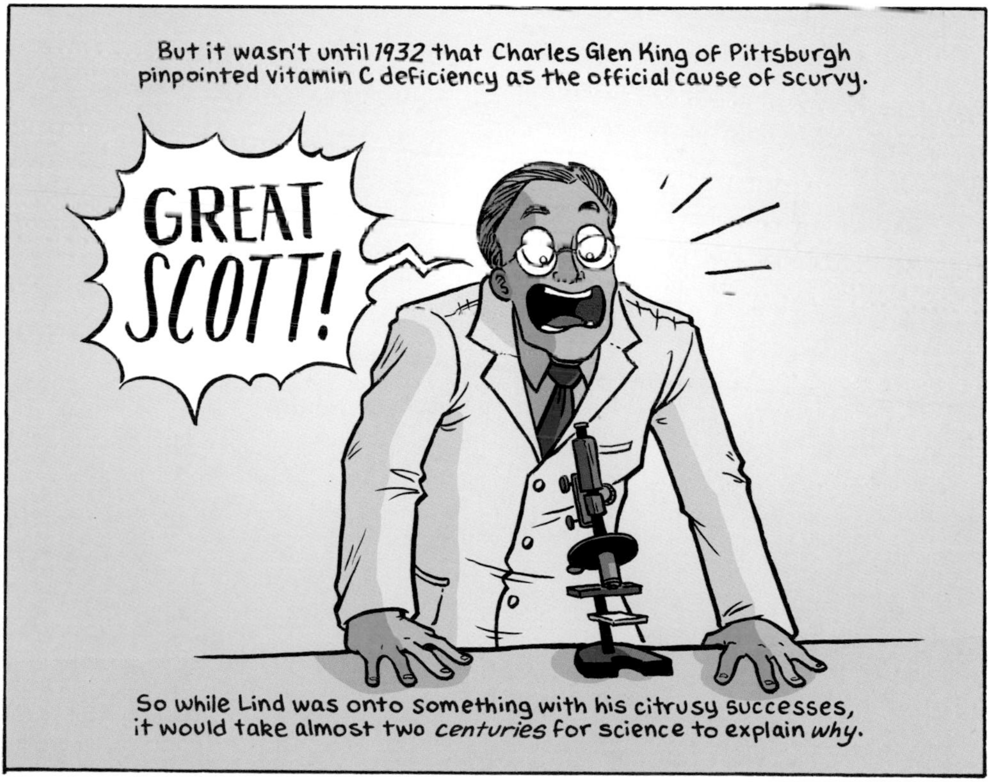
But it wasn't until 1932 that Charles Glen King of Pittsburgh pinpointed vitamin C deficiency as the official cause of scurvy.
GREAT SCOTT!
So while Lind was onto something with his citrusy successes, it would take almost two centuries for science to explain why.

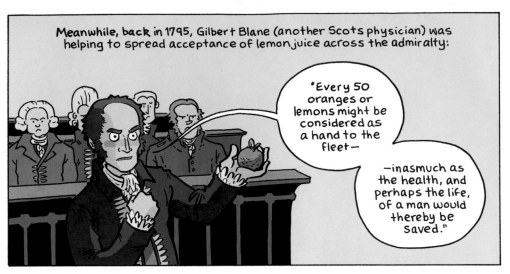

Meanwhile, back in 1795, Gilbert Blane (another Scots physician) was helping to spread acceptance of lemon juice across the admiralty:

"Every 50 oranges or lemons might be considered as a hand to the fleet—

—inasmuch as the health, and perhaps the life, of a man would thereby be saved."

Well that certainly **sounds** convincing.

I suppose we should get some lemons.

...Where **do** lemons come from?

Uh... Sicily?

TO SICILY!

So we're gonna need, like...all of these.

Um, okay?

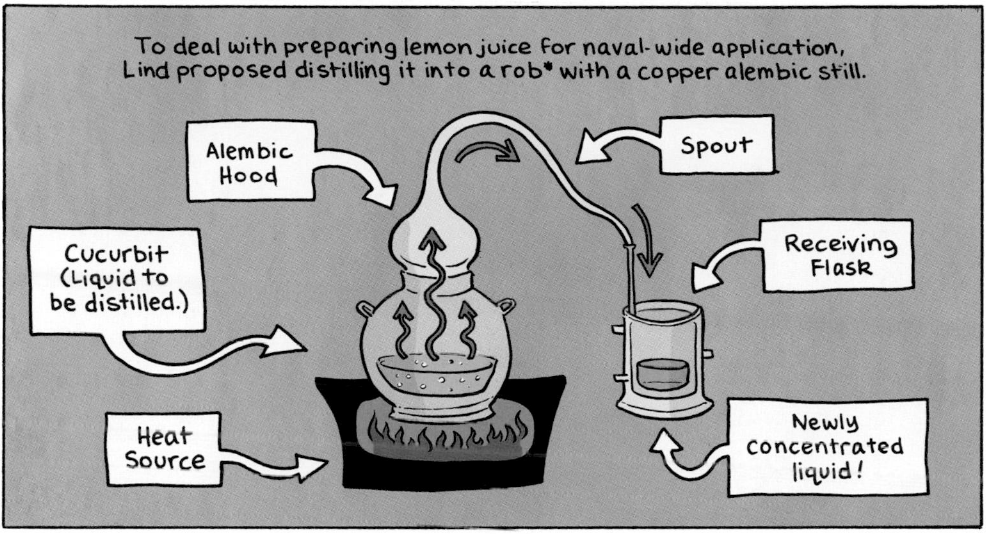
To deal with preparing lemon juice for naval-wide application, Lind proposed distilling it into a rob* with a copper alembic still.
Alembic Hood
Spout
Cucurbit (Liquid to be distilled.)
Receiving Flask
Heat Source
Newly concentrated liquid!

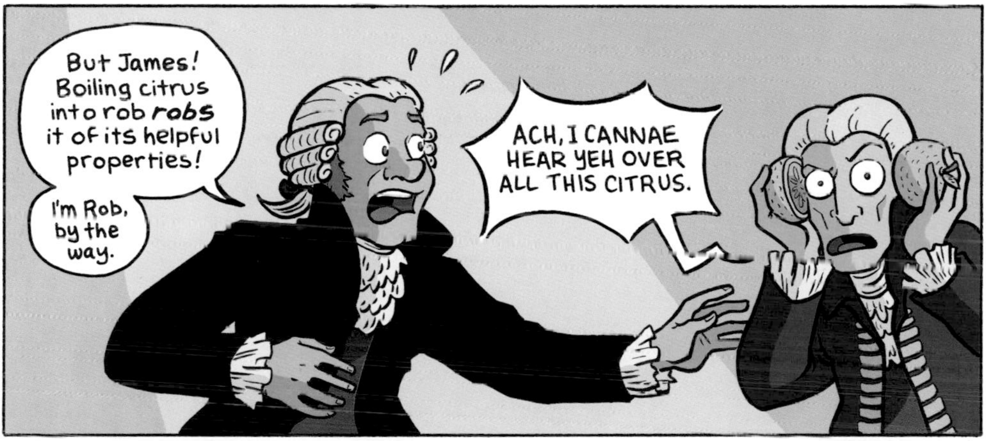
But James! Boiling citrus into rob *robs* it of its helpful properties!
I'm Rob, by the way.
ACH, I CANNAE HEAR YEH OVER ALL THIS CITRUS.

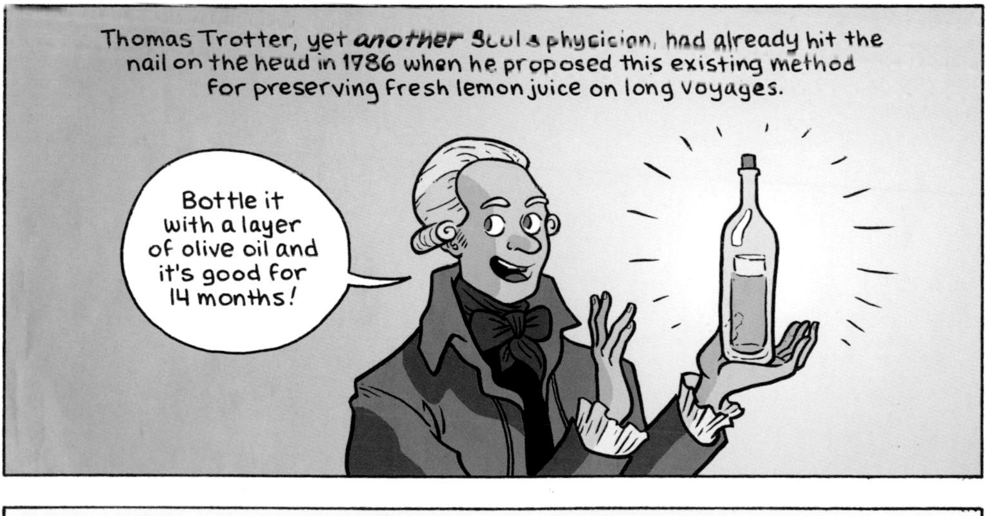
Thomas Trotter, yet *another* Scots physician, had already hit the nail on the head in 1786 when he proposed this existing method for preserving fresh lemon juice on long voyages.
Bottle it with a layer of olive oil and it's good for 14 months!

*A rob is a concentrate produced by boiling liquid and siphoning off the distillation.

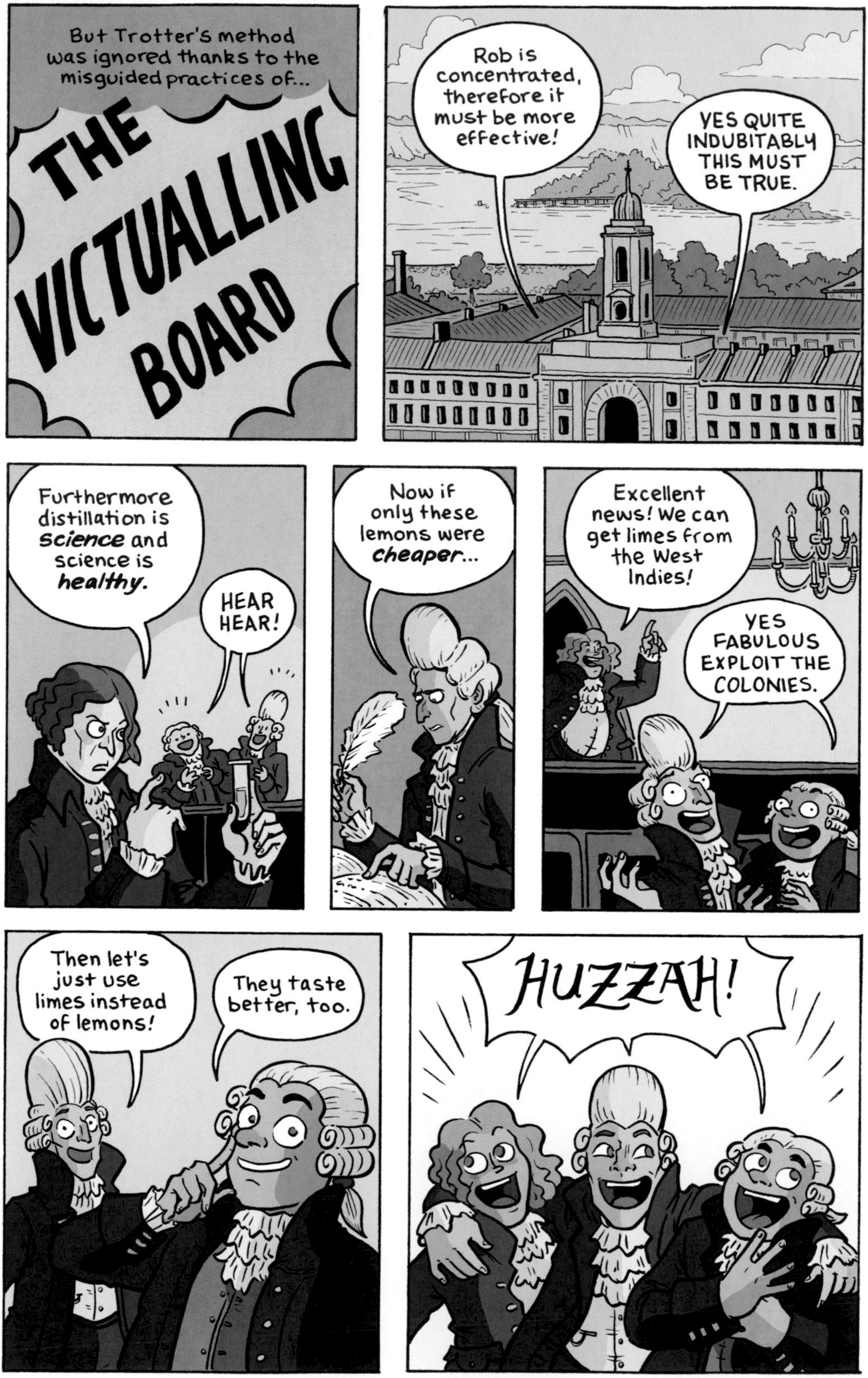
But Trotter's method was ignored thanks to the misguided practices of...
THE VICTUALLING BOARD
Rob is concentrated, therefore it must be more effective!
YES QUITE INDUBITABLY THIS MUST BE TRUE.
Furthermore distillation is *science* and science is *healthy*.
HEAR HEAR!
Now if only these lemons were *cheaper*...
Excellent news! We can get limes from the West Indies!
YES FABULOUS EXPLOIT THE COLONIES.
Then let's just use limes instead of lemons!
They taste better, too.
HUZZAH!

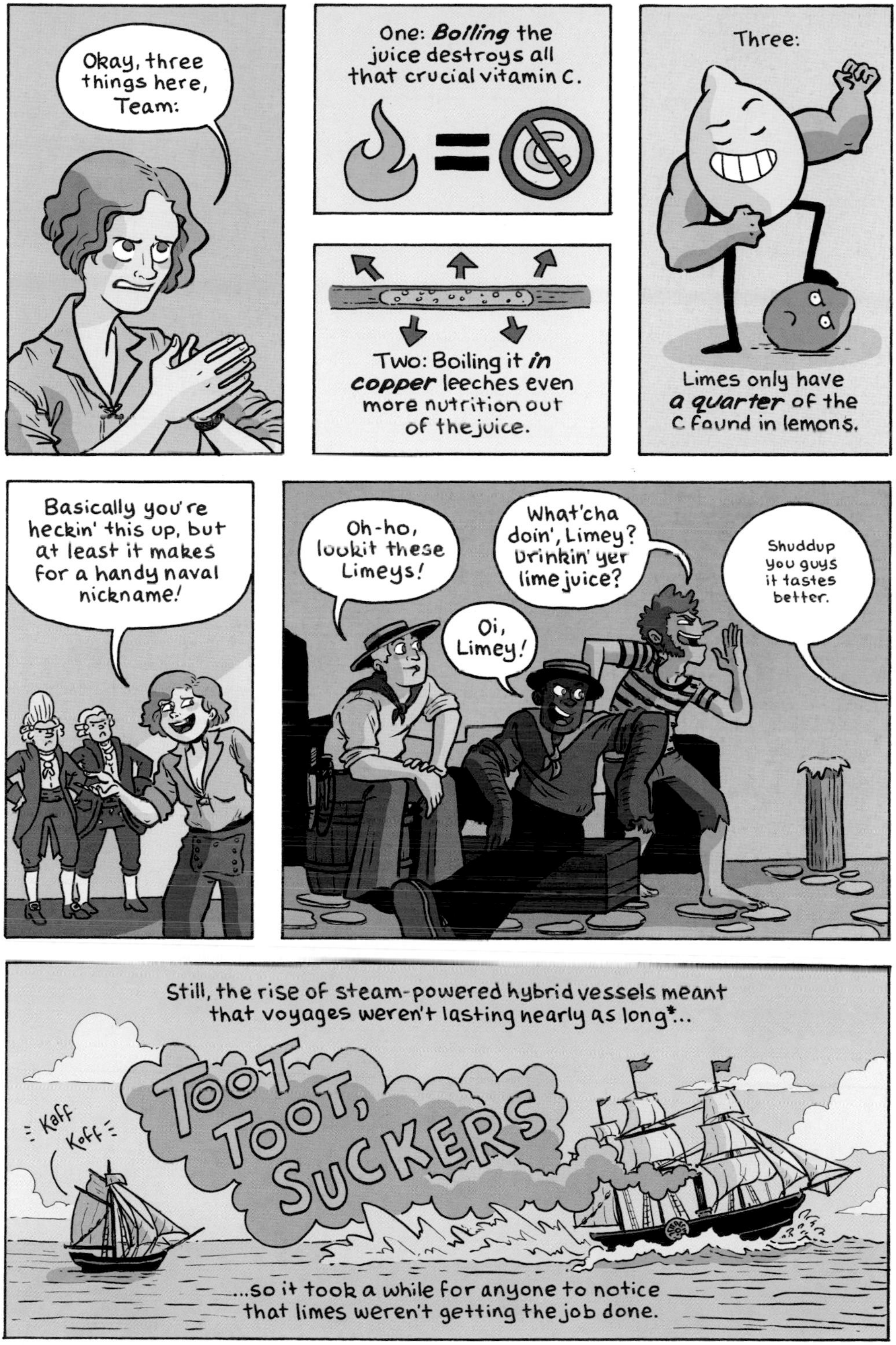
Okay, three things here, Team:
One: **Boiling** the juice destroys all that crucial vitamin C.
Two: Boiling it ***in copper*** leeches even more nutrition out of the juice.
Three:
Limes only have ***a quarter*** of the C found in lemons.
Basically you're heckin' this up, but at least it makes for a handy naval nickname!
Oh-ho, lookit these Limeys!
What'cha doin', Limey? Drinkin' yer lime juice?
Oi, Limey!
Shuddup you guys it tastes better.
Still, the rise of steam-powered hybrid vessels meant that voyages weren't lasting nearly as long*...
Kaff Kaff
TOOT TOOT, SUCKERS
...so it took a while for anyone to notice that limes weren't getting the job done.

*Unless you were a whaler, in which case you could be at sea for **five years** or more!

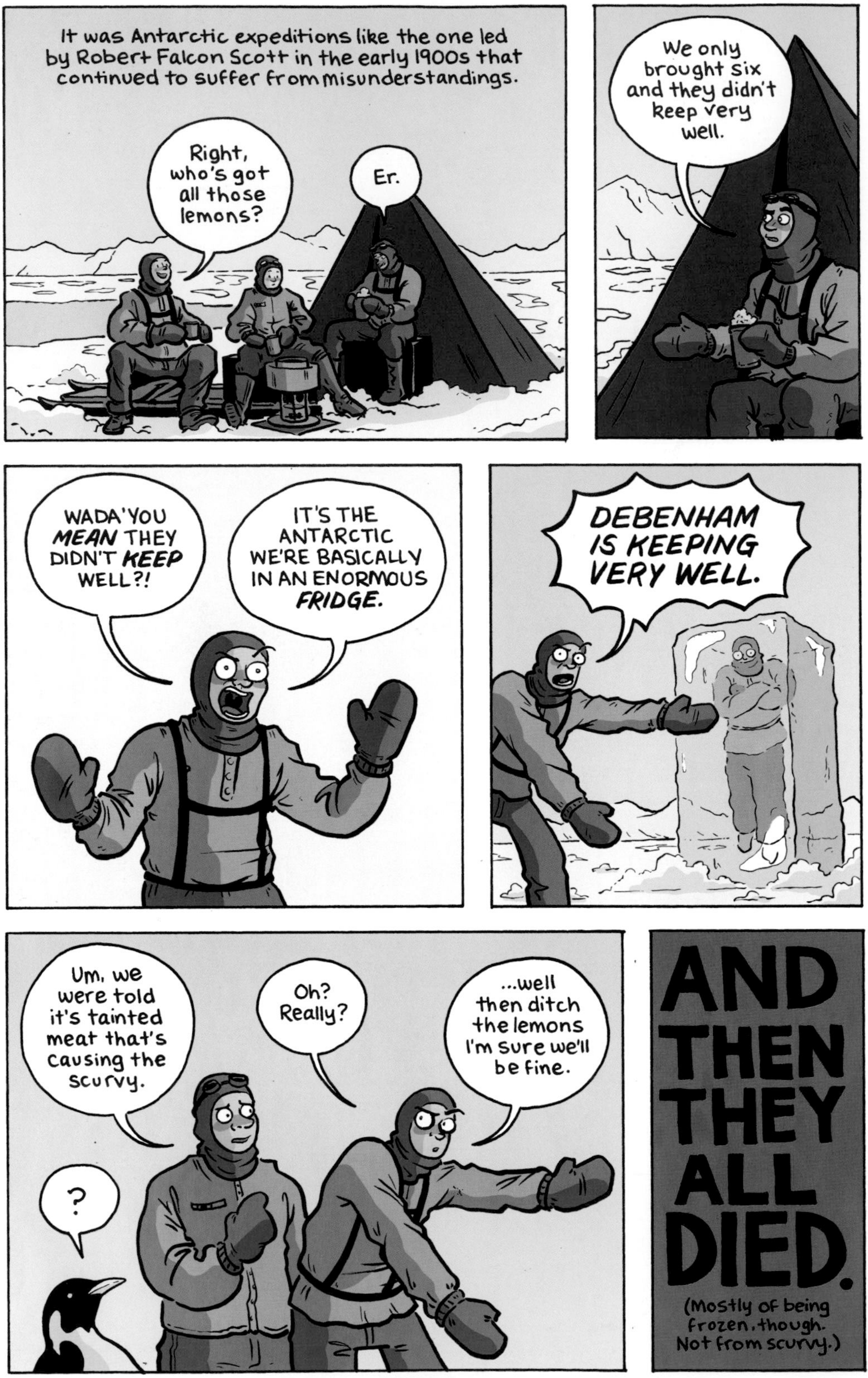
It was Antarctic expeditions like the one led by Robert Falcon Scott in the early 1900s that continued to suffer from misunderstandings.
Right, who's got all those lemons?
Er.
We only brought six and they didn't keep very well.
WADA'YOU MEAN THEY DIDN'T KEEP WELL?!
IT'S THE ANTARCTIC WE'RE BASICALLY IN AN ENORMOUS FRIDGE.
DEBENHAM IS KEEPING VERY WELL.
Um, we were told it's tainted meat that's causing the scurvy.
Oh? Really?
...well then ditch the lemons I'm sure we'll be fine.
?
AND THEN THEY ALL DIED.
(Mostly of being frozen, though. Not from scurvy.)

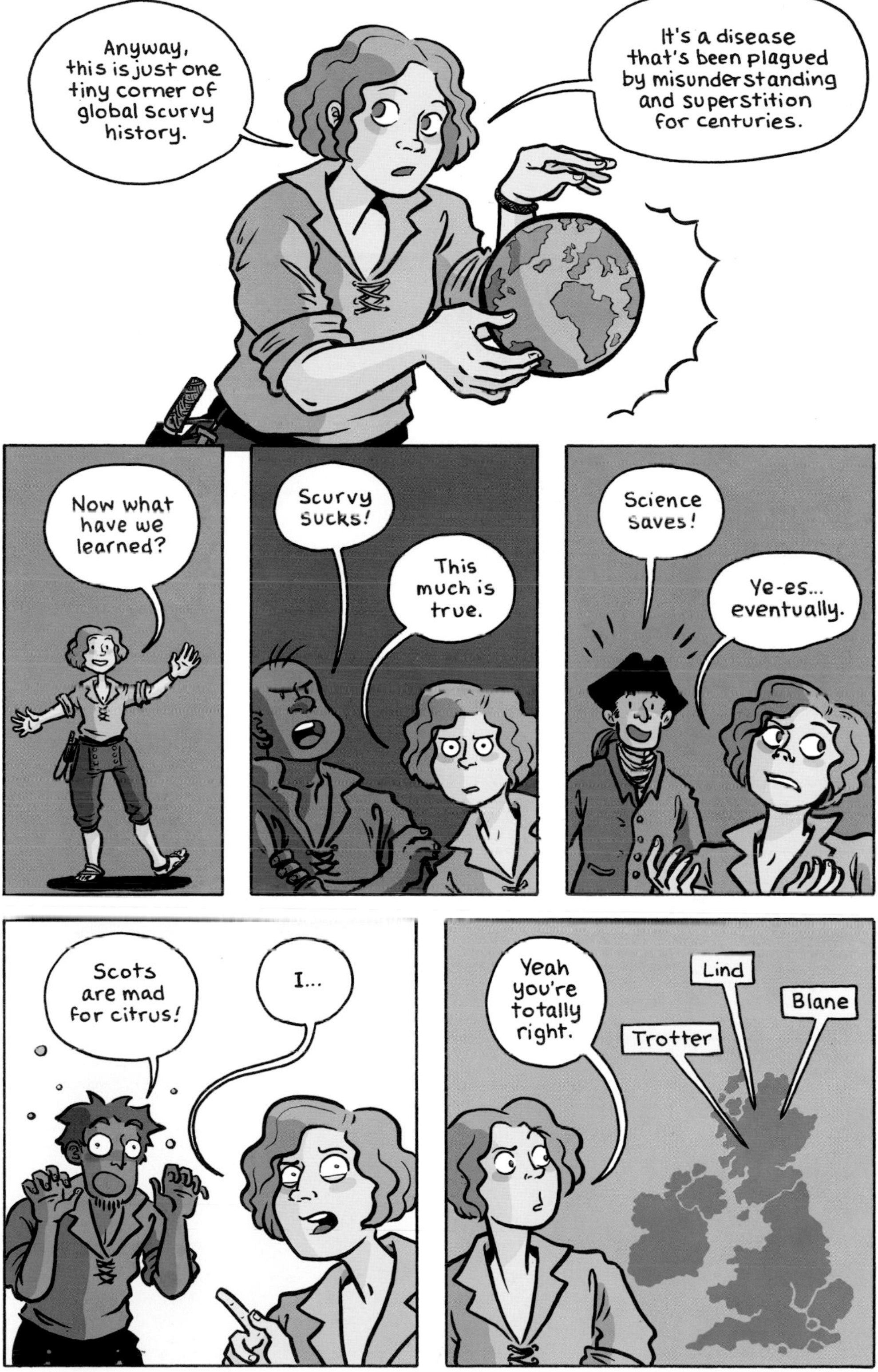
Anyway, this is just one tiny corner of global scurvy history.
It's a disease that's been plagued by misunderstanding and superstition for centuries.
Now what have we learned?
Scurvy sucks!
This much is true.
Science saves!
Ye-es... eventually.
Scots are mad for citrus!
I...
Yeah you're totally right.
Lind
Blane
Trotter

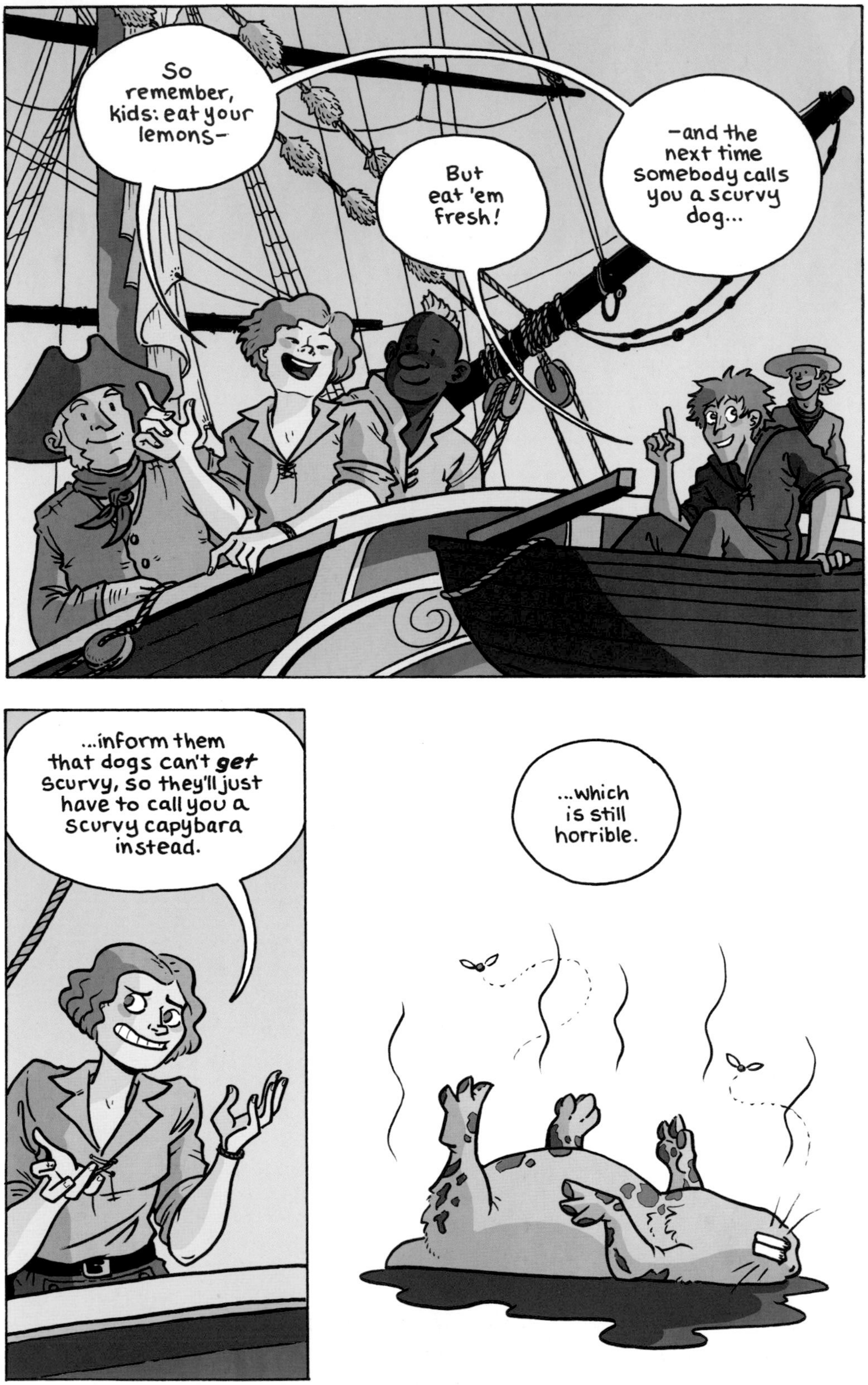
So remember, kids: eat your lemons–
But eat 'em fresh!
–and the next time somebody calls you a scurvy dog...
...inform them that dogs can't *get* scurvy, so they'll just have to call you a scurvy capybara instead.
...which is still horrible.

SCURVY

Afterword

I had a wonderful time researching scurvy with Lucy for this comic, and since comics are often distillations of larger narratives, I'd feel remiss if I did not add a few additional thoughts.

Doing the research we discovered that the topic of scurvy is vast; ocean vast. The history of vitamin deficiencies provides an excellent view of the history of science. In the treatment of just one disease I see humanity move from sawing wood and Hoping That Worked to knowing the nature of a disease that has plagued us for all time.

The importance of scurvy in the development of clinical trials is at once remarkable and not terribly important at all. In *A treatise of the Scurvy* Lind pays virtually no attention to the trial itself, taking a mere four pages in a 450-page book. It is important to remember that Lind's thinking was not based on the knowledge that we have today. The scientific method was not fully developed and medical advances were frustrated by not knowing basic facts. Still, the "fair trial" of scurvy treatments by Lind is a good example of the Enlightenment thinking of the time and was a move in the right direction. That's really the story of scurvy; moving in the right direction without ever knowing it. I am struck by just how often we came right to the edge of understanding this disease only to wander away from the answer because of misunderstanding the question.

To complicate matters, the introduction of fresh foods into the diet of sailors (as would occur during a port call on an island) could temporarily cure cases of scurvy and muddle scientific observation of potential cures. The erroneous correlation between an absence of terra firma and scurvy even led sailors to bury their shipmates up to the neck upon reaching land, then assume that the restorative properties of the soil would cure their afflictions.

I spent a great deal of time looking at the food and eating habits of sailors in 18th- and 19th-century British naval vessels and came away with far more questions than answers. Only one answer was made quite clear to me: the food was very dull. I cannot imagine staring down one's 2000th bowl of Pease Porridge in a row. I became very grateful for refrigeration and the bounty of foods brought by modern commerce.

Capybara Nelson

Even on a Very Long Ocean Voyage today it is reasonable that you will see more than three types of food. Ultimately, there's a huge story lurking in what the Victualling Board bought and how that weaves empire, economics, class, and dinner together.

Due to space constraints, we skirted the topic of modern scurvy, even though it remains a huge affliction for many underserved populations around the world. Scurvy in very young children was a huge problem in the early 20th century in the U.S. and Canada due to the introduction of infant formula which did not contain enough vitamin C. The most recent large-scale scurvy problem occurred in 1982 among Ethiopian nomadic refugees in Somalia. Since the vast majority of their vitamin C was originally delivered by camel's milk—a resource no longer available to them in refugee camps—there was a significant outbreak. Much like piracy, we jest about the historical precedents of these issues, but it is worth noting that they remain hazardous to many populations today.

Ultimately, this disease affected so many generations of sailors that it appears in every story, every account of exploration and danger, and every ship's log. I do not wish to learn naval history merely as a matter of fleets, maps, and dates—there's room enough for that in learning. By letting one's research branch out from scurvy, you're never too far away from a sailor's life, and walking around with the crew contextualizes what can become a very heady and far-off topic.

I can do that walking, of course, because I do not have scorbutic lesions about my legs and torso.

Eriq Nelson

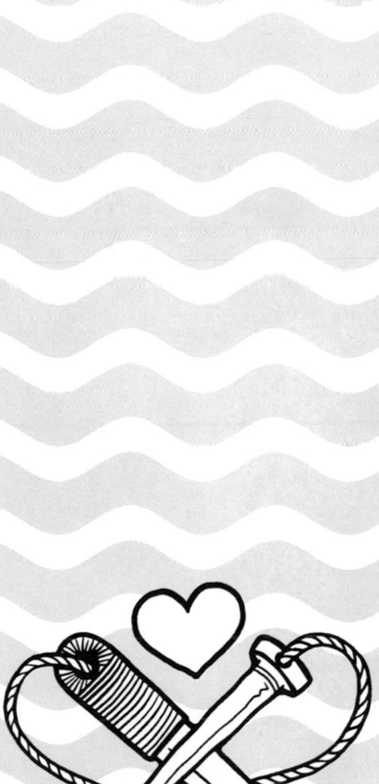

THE SCURVY *Rogues*

GUEST ART GALLERY

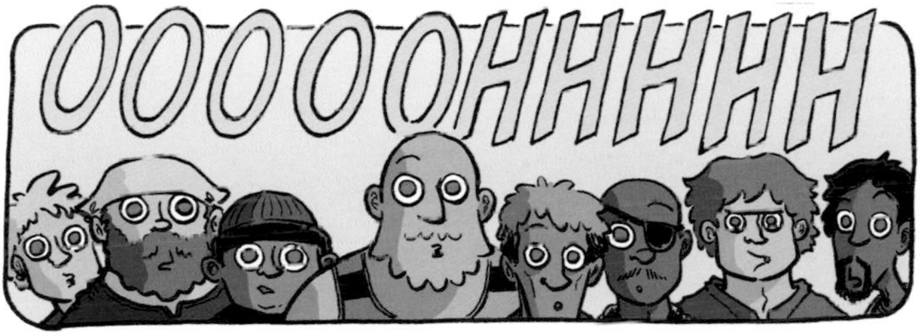
OOOOOHHHHH

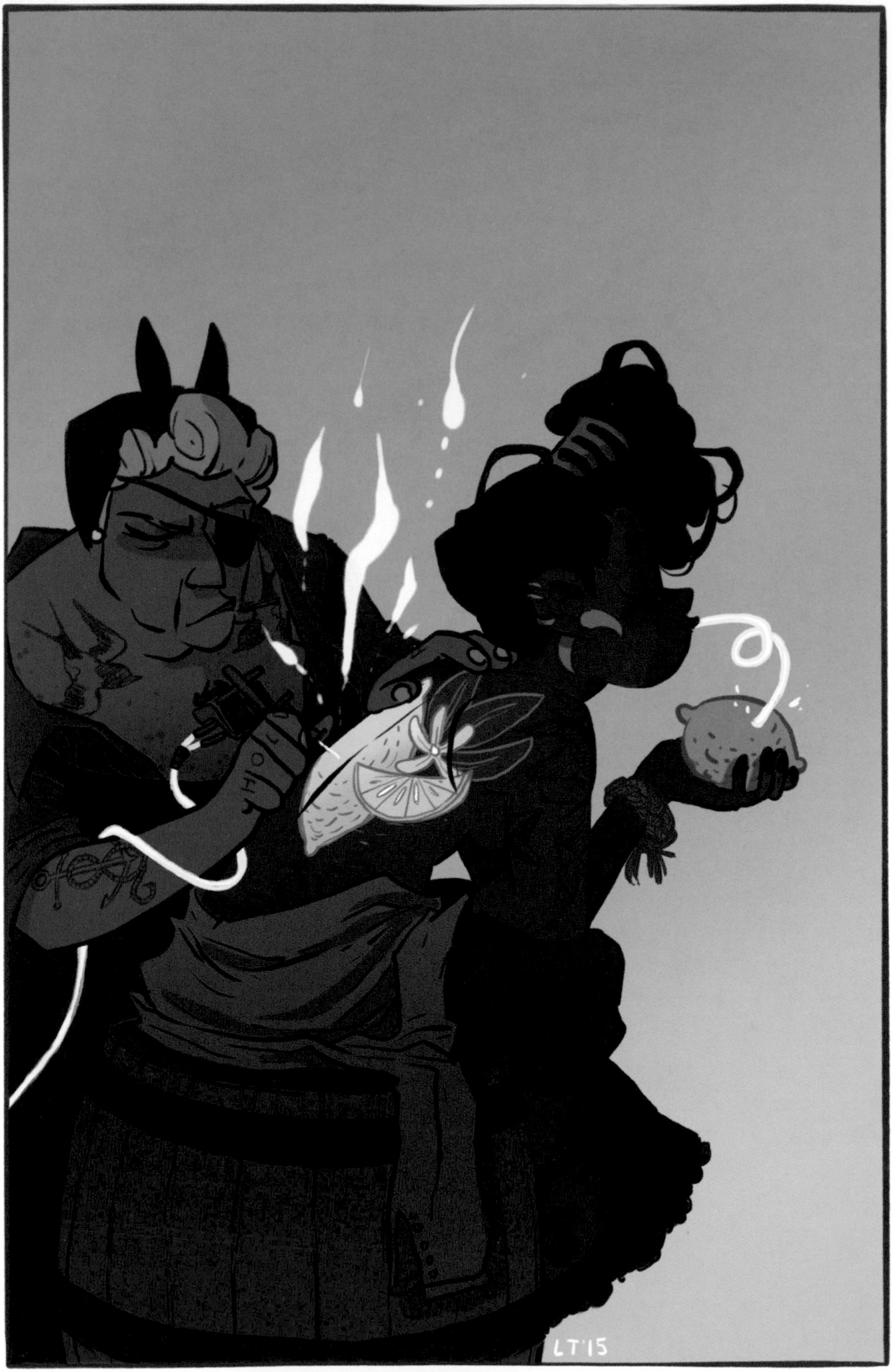
LT'15

Lissa Treiman » @lbtreiman « lissabt.tumblr.com

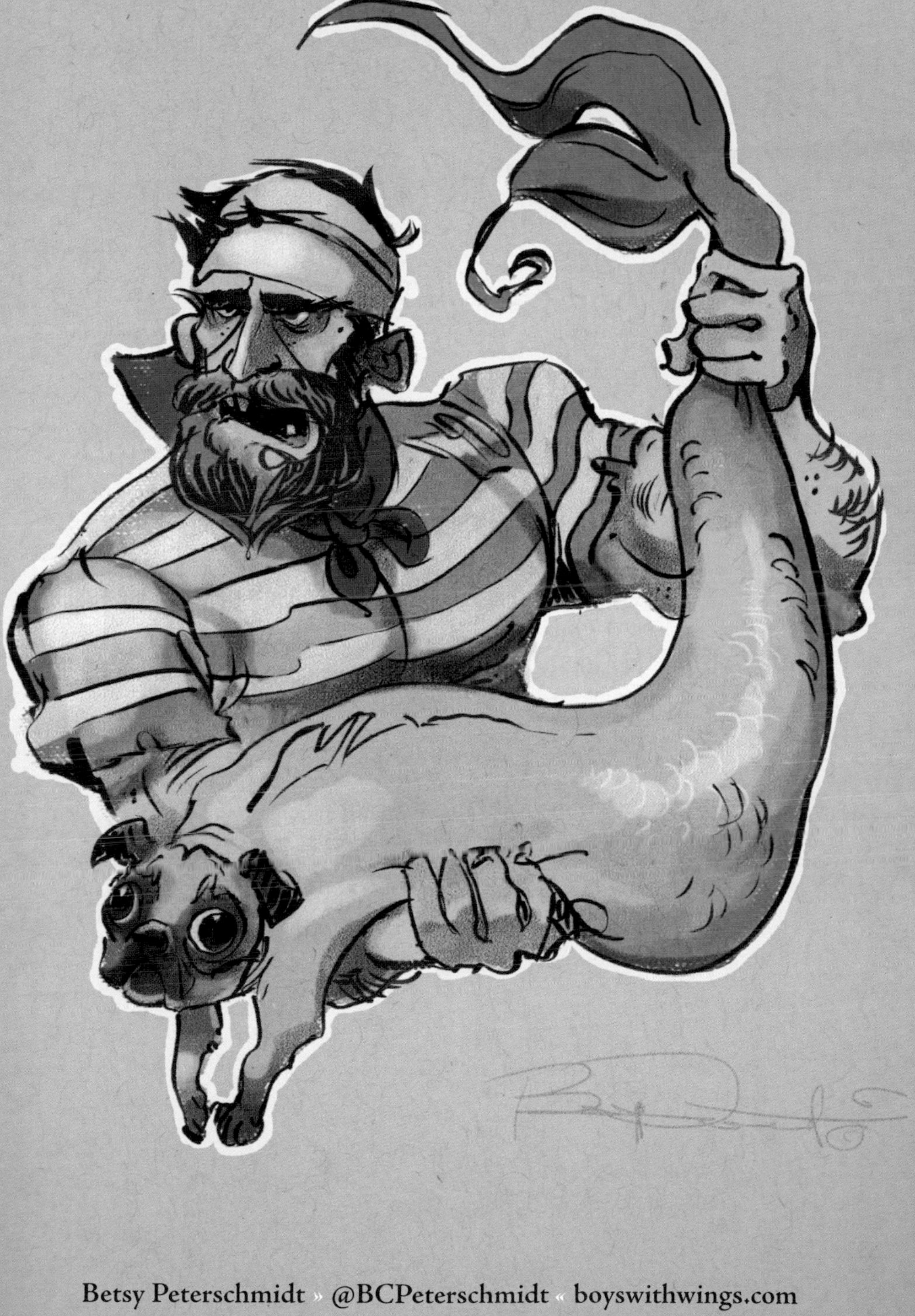

Betsy Peterschmidt » @BCPeterschmidt « boyswithwings.com

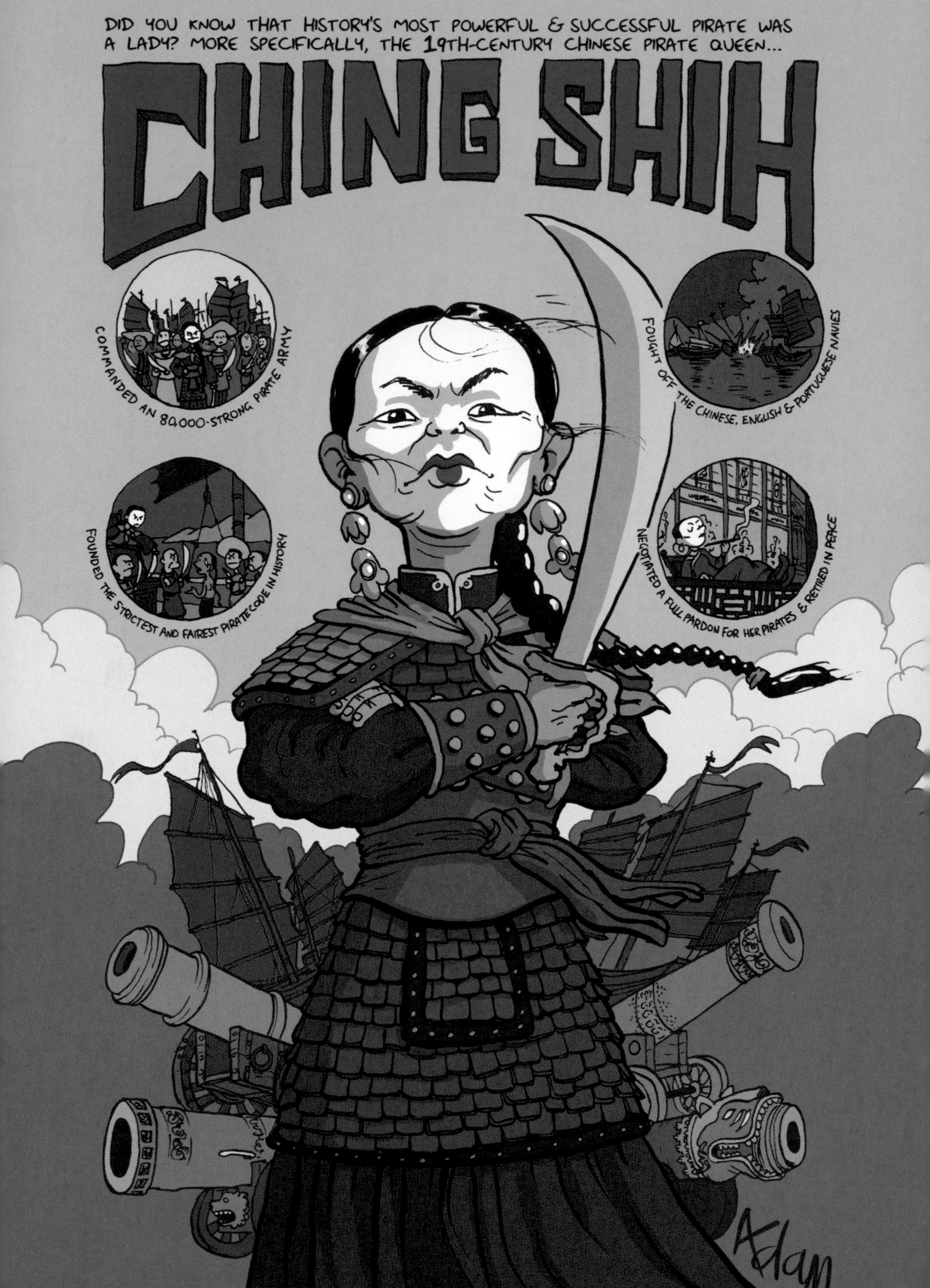
DID YOU KNOW THAT HISTORY'S MOST POWERFUL & SUCCESSFUL PIRATE WAS A LADY? MORE SPECIFICALLY, THE 19TH-CENTURY CHINESE PIRATE QUEEN...
CHING SHIH
COMMANDED AN 80,000-STRONG PIRATE ARMY
FOUGHT OFF THE CHINESE, ENGLISH & PORTUGUESE NAVIES
FOUNDED THE STRICTEST AND FAIREST PIRATE CODE IN HISTORY
NEGOTIATED A FULL PARDON FOR HER PIRATES & RETIRED IN PEACE
Adam

Adam T. Murphy @Adam_T_Murphy adammurphy.com

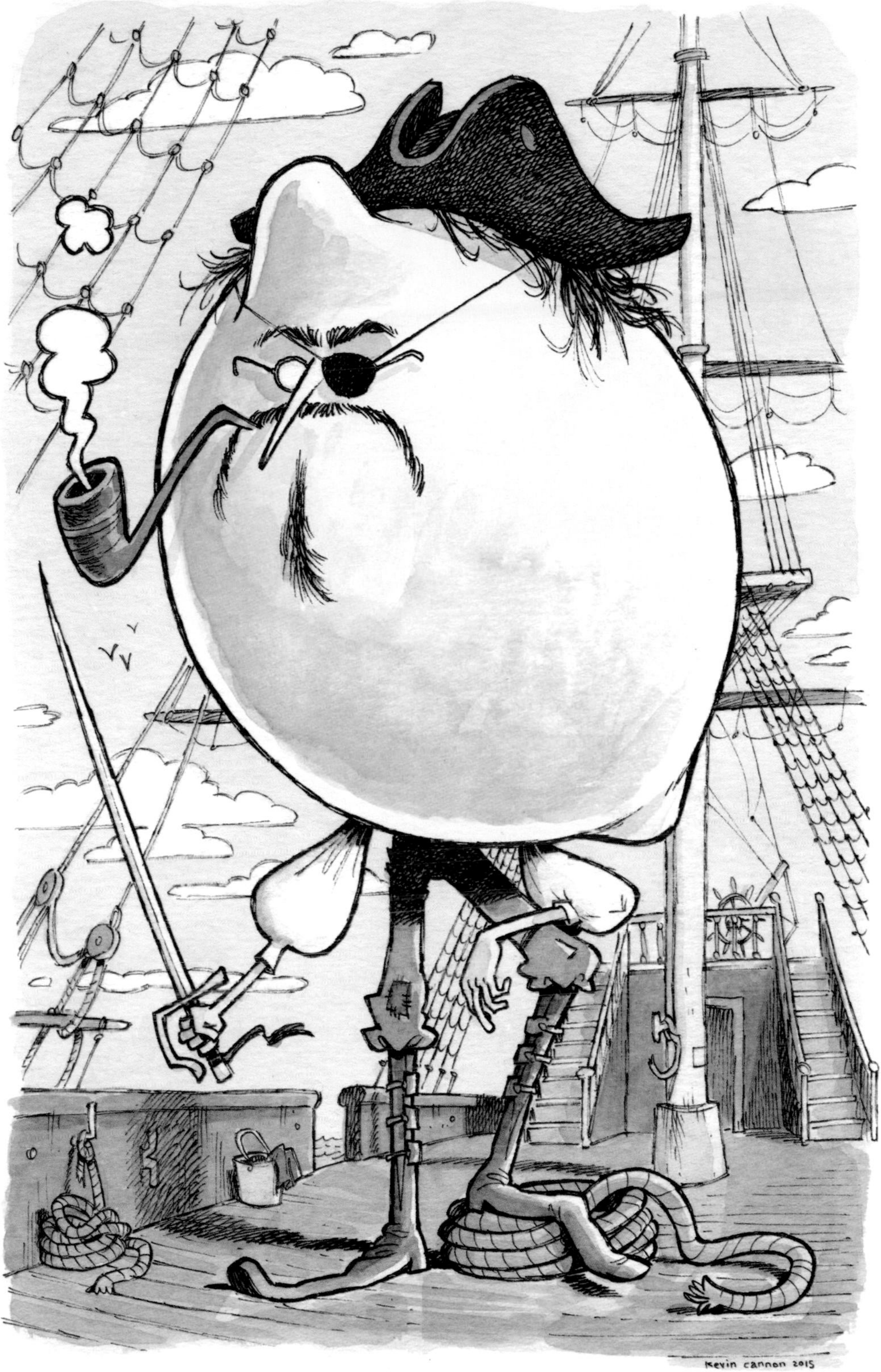
Kevin cannon 2015

Kevin Cannon » **@beardhero** « **kevincannon.org**

NEARLY SEVEN
Important Figures
IN THE HISTORY OF
SCURVY

ALBERT SZENT-GYÖRGYI

Nobel Prize-winning discoverer of Vitamin C

JAMES LIND

Developed theory that citrus fruits cure scurvy

HIPPOCRATES

Described scurvy symptoms among ancient Greeks

SIR THOMAS BARLOW

Known for his research on infantile scurvy

DOMINIQUE JEAN LARREY

Curbed French Army scurvy epidemic with horse meat

CHARLES GLEN KING

Proved connection between ascorbic acid and scurvy

Ben Towle » @ben_towle benzilla.com

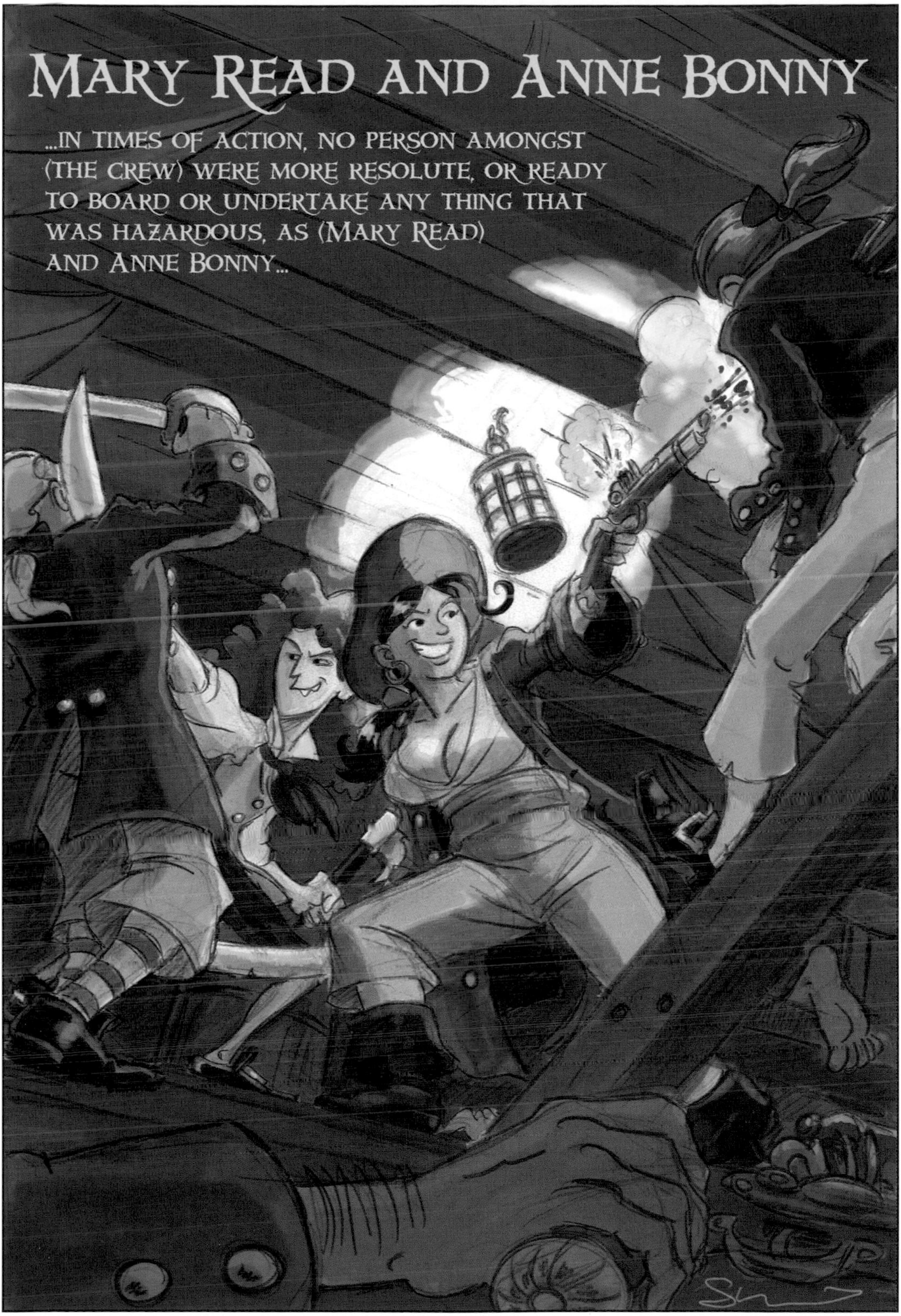
MARY READ AND ANNE BONNY
...IN TIMES OF ACTION, NO PERSON AMONGST (THE CREW) WERE MORE RESOLUTE, OR READY TO BOARD OR UNDERTAKE ANY THING THAT WAS HAZARDOUS, AS (MARY READ) AND ANNE BONNY...

Steve LeCouilliard » @stevelecoui « stevelecouilliard.deviantart.com

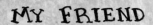

MY FRIEND
PAUL WALKER *NOT THE ACTOR
WHO HAD REAL-LIFE SCURVY IN 2007!

SELF DESCRIBED "SHUT-IN" AND PICKY EATER

ROMANTICISES SUFFERING

BLEEDING GUMS

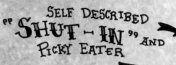

No one was surprised, I eat trash every day.

SORES

We all thought it was Chicken Pox.

PAUL'S MOM

PRIMARY DIET

PASTA

CHEESE

TUNA

MEAT

OLD SCARS OPENING UP →

← NOT GREAT

THE CURE

BASICALLY HE JUST DRANK SUNNY-D UNTIL HIS SCARS STOPPED BLEEDING.

SO THEY CALLED PAUL'S AUNT WHO IS A DOCTOR.

It's like chicken pox but he's vaccinated for that

HMM... CHECK HIS GUMS.

HMMMMM

They're pretty red...

YOUR SON HAS SCURVY.

MAKE HIM DRINK SOME VITAMIN C NOW!

EPILOGUE: PAUL GOT SCURVY AGAIN IN HIS FRESHMAN YEAR OF COLLEGE. HE LEARNED HIS LESSON THAT TIME. NOW, DUE TO DIET CHANGE AND THE WOMEN IN HIS LIFE, PAUL IS FULLY RECOVERED AND VERY HANDSOME!

PAUL 2015

© ISABELLA ROTMAN 2015

Isabella Rotman » @IsabellaRotman « isabellarotman.com

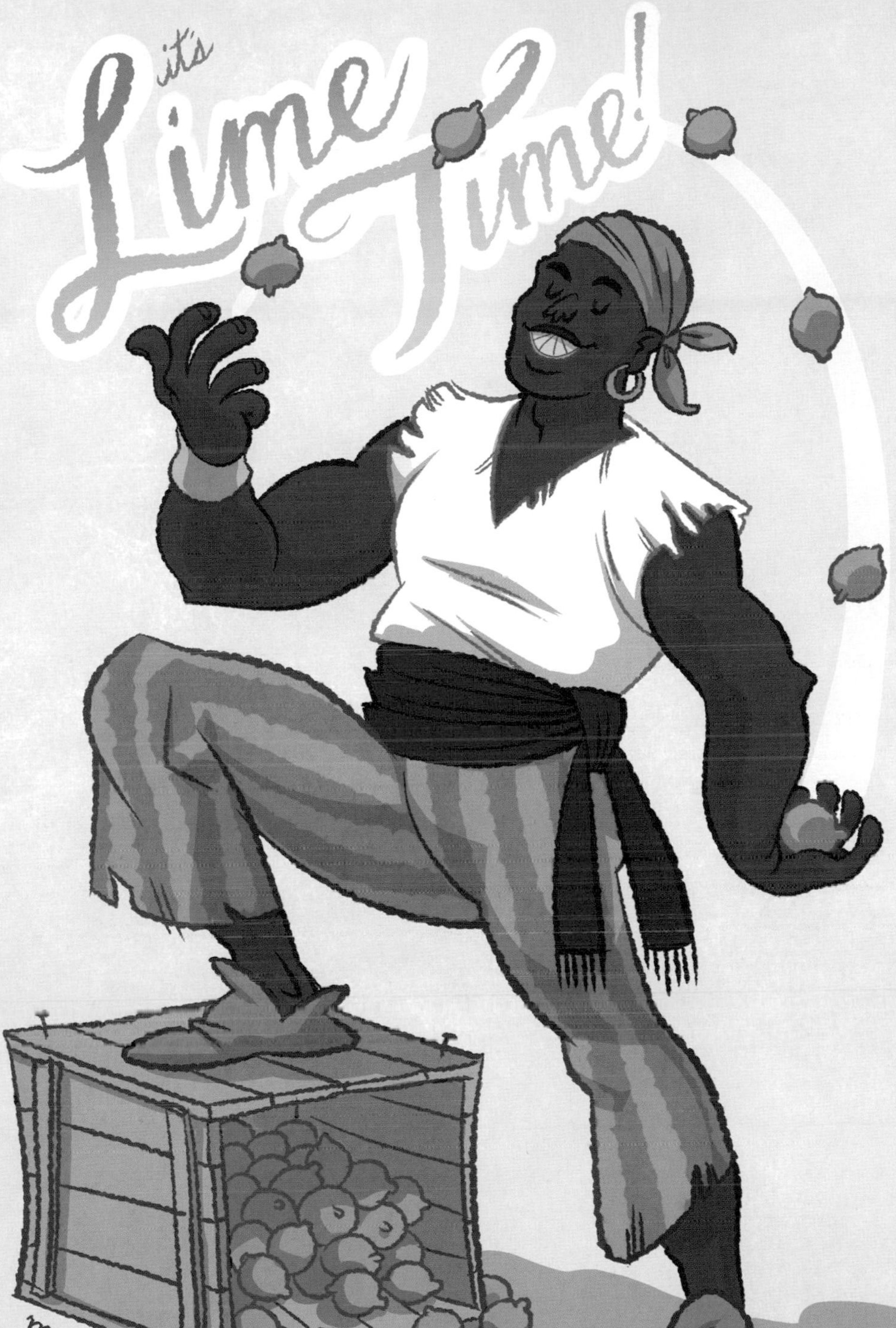
it's
Lime
Time!
meconis

Dylan Meconis » @dmeconis « dylanmeconis.com

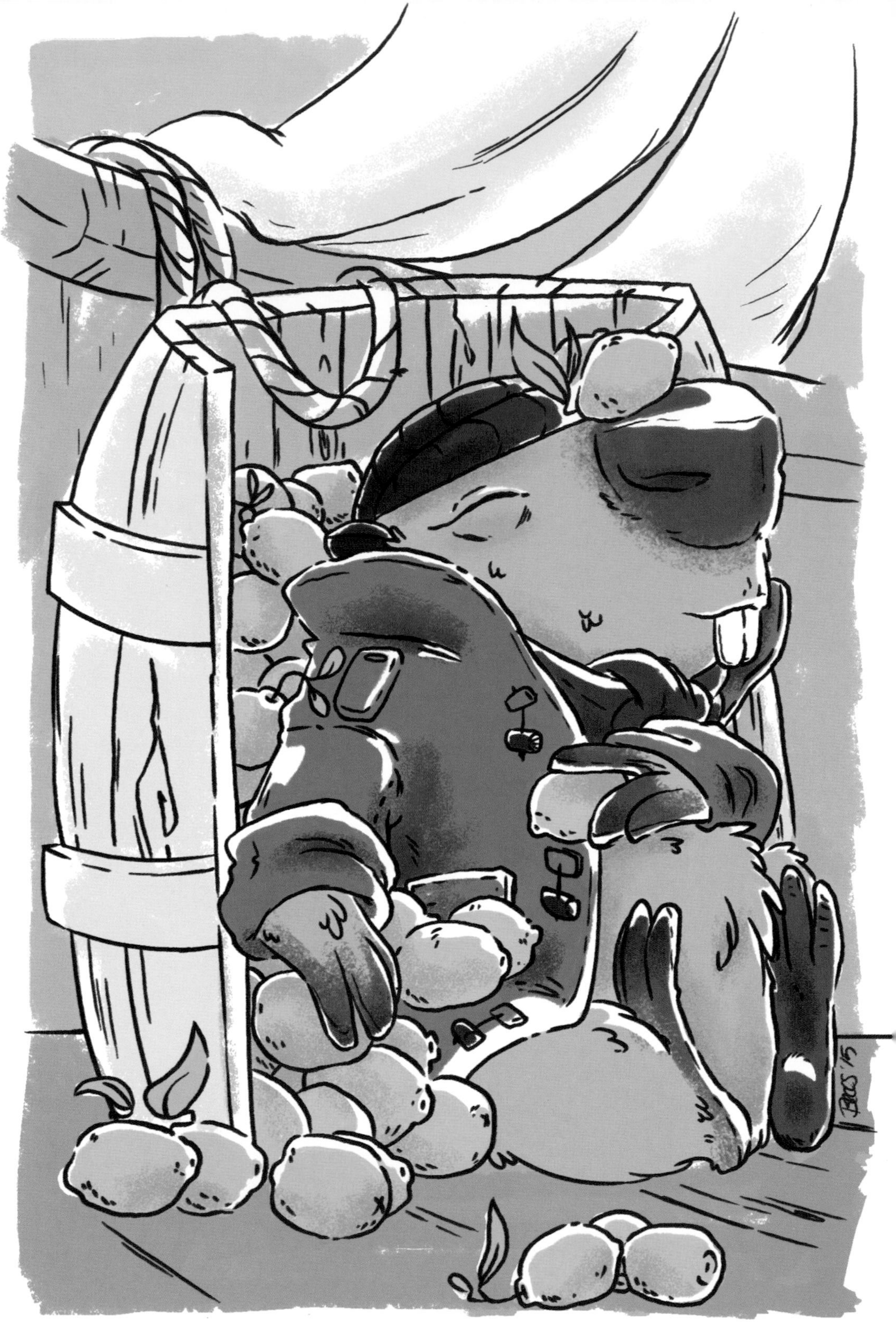

Beccy David » @beccydavid « becja.tumblr.com

THE END

GRATITUDE

Given that this book spans the first five years of my career in comics, I'd have a hard time thanking every person who has contributed to its creation. However, the following names are particularly deserving of recognition:

The educators and students at **The Center for Cartoon Studies**, particularly **Alec Longstreth** and **Beth Hetland**, who facilitated my first foray into making comics during a five-day workshop back in 2010.

⚓

Grays Harbor Historical Seaport Authority and the sailors who welcomed me into their midst while crewing on the *Lady Washington*.

⚓

My comrades at **Periscope Studio** for their keen eyes and terrible jokes.

⚓

Frank Turner for allowing me to use the lyrics from his gorgeous song "Sailor's Boots" as an intro to Issue 3.

⚓

The **many kind readers** who have taken the time to tell me their sailing stories, introduce me to their boat-mad relatives, and drop a line when they've turned to a life at sea after reading these stories—your support makes this all so magical.

⚓

And, of course, **my family** for their boundless enthusiasm, love, and lunacy.